ideals

All Holidays
COOKBOOK

CASTLE
BOOKS

Published by
CASTLE BOOKS
A Division of
BOOK SALES, INC.
110 Enterprise Avenue
Secaucus, New Jersey 07094

Introduction

Holidays and entertaining go together, and this cookbook provides you with new and interesting food ideas to make those special occasions even more memorable. Ranging from picnic simplicity to party elegance, the recipes and suggestions are equally good anytime.

There are tips for giving a successful party as well as varied and unique menu plans. Foods for all the major holidays throughout the year are featured such as Valentine's Day, Easter, Mother's Day, Father's Day, Thanksgiving, and Christmas. Also included are recipes for seasonal celebrations including a springtime luncheon, summer cookout and harvest get-together, as well as party ideas for youngsters. You'll never have to wonder again what to prepare for that special luncheon, Sunday brunch, or graduation party. Your guests will ask for the recipes!

Enjoy entertaining family and friends with tasty and attractive fare and await with confidence the compliments that are sure to follow.

ISBN 0-89009-478-0

COPYRIGHT © MCMLXXIV BY IDEALS PUBLISHING CORP.
ALL RIGHTS RESERVED
THIS EDITION IS PUBLISHED BY CASTLE BOOKS,
A DIVISION OF BOOK SALES, INC.,
BY ARRANGEMENT WITH IDEALS PUBLISHING CORPORATION.
a b c d e f g h
CASTLE 1981 EDITION
MANUFACTURED IN THE UNITED STATES OF AMERICA

Contents

New Year Party

Lemon Champagne Punch

Makes 50 servings.

4 6-ounce cans frozen lemonade concentrate
4 6-ounce cans frozen pineapple juice
1½ quarts water
2 quarts ginger ale, chilled
1 quart sparkling water, chilled
1 bottle (⅘ quart) dry champagne, chilled

Combine juices and water. Chill, covered. Before serving, add ginger ale and sparkling water; pour over ice cubes in a large punch bowl. Pour chilled champagne over punch and stir gently.

New Year's Eve Party Cheese Ball

2 8-ounce packages cream cheese
¼ pound blue cheese
½ pound extra-sharp Cheddar cheese, grated
1 tablespoon Worcestershire sauce
1 teaspoon cayenne pepper
½ teaspoon salt
½ teaspoon onion powder
½ teaspoon garlic powder
1 cup chopped pecans

Allow cheeses to reach room temperature; combine in a mixing bowl. Beat until well blended. Add Worcestershire sauce, cayenne pepper, salt, onion powder, and garlic powder. Add ½ cup of the chopped pecans. Chill. Shape into a ball and roll ball in remaining pecans. Chill thoroughly. Serve with assorted crackers and fresh fruits such as seedless grapes, apple and pear slices. Freeze, if desired.

Holiday Spinach Salad

5 slices bacon, fried and crumbled, reserve 2 tablespoons fat
3 tablespoons lemon juice
2 tablespoons salad oil
1 tablespoon sugar
½ teaspoon salt
½ teaspoon ground tarragon
1 pound spinach, washed and torn into bite-size pieces
1 cup sliced green onions
1½ cups celery slices
Sliced orange sections

In a jar combine the bacon, 2 tablespoons bacon fat, lemon juice, salad oil, sugar, salt, and tarragon. Shake vigorously until all ingredients are well combined. Combine spinach, onions, celery, and orange sections. Pour dressing over all; toss until well coated.

Note: If desired, use half the amount of spinach and add other salad greens and tomatoes.

Auld Lang Syne Casserole

Makes 6 servings.

3 pounds chicken, cooked and cut up
1 cup chopped celery, cooked in chicken broth
1 cup rice, cooked in chicken broth
2 tablespoons minced onion
Salt to taste
1 10¾-ounce can cream of chicken soup
¾ cup mayonnaise
½ cup slivered almonds
1 cup cornflakes, crushed
4 tablespoons margarine, melted

Mix all ingredients together, except cornflakes and margarine, in a casserole. Cover with cornflakes; drizzle on margarine. Bake at 350° for 30 minutes.

Peach Delight

3 egg whites
1 cup sugar
¼ teaspoon baking powder
1 teaspoon vanilla extract
½ cup pecans, finely chopped
½ cup finely crushed soda crackers

Beat egg whites stiff. Fold in sugar, baking powder, vanilla, pecans, and soda crackers. Pour into a buttered 11 x 7-inch pan. Bake at 325° for 30 minutes. Cool.

Topping

½ pint whipping cream, whipped
1 tablespoon confectioners' sugar
1 large can sliced peaches, well drained

Add sugar to whipped cream. Fold in peaches. Pour over cracker mixture and refrigerate overnight.

French Chocolate

Makes 4 servings.

2½ squares bitter chocolate
 1 cup water
 ½ cup sugar
   Salt to taste
 1 teaspoon vanilla extract
 1 cup whipping cream, whipped
 4 cups heated milk

Cook the chocolate with water until thick, stirring to prevent sticking. Add sugar and salt. Bring to a boil; remove from heat. Cool. Add vanilla. Fold in whipped cream. Makes about 2½ cups sauce. Place a generous spoonful of sauce in each of 4 serving cups. Refrigerate additional sauce for future use. Add hot milk to fill cup. Stir until mixed.

Nibble Mix

 ½ pound butter, melted
 3 tablespoons Worcestershire sauce
 4 cups each Rice Chex, Wheat Chex, Cheerios
 4 cups pretzel sticks
 1 can mixed nuts
 1 teaspoon garlic salt
 1 teaspoon onion salt

Place butter in a baking dish; stir in Worcestershire sauce. Add dry cereals, pretzel sticks, and nuts. Sprinkle with the garlic and onion salts; mix well. Bake at 225° for 1 hour, stirring occasionally.

Sombrero Snacks

 2 ounces Cheddar cheese
 1 mild chili pepper, diced
24 taco-flavored tortilla chips
   Bean dip

Cut cheese into 24 pieces. Arrange tortilla chips on a baking sheet. Place 1 teaspoon bean dip on each chip and top with cheese and chili pepper. Place 4 to 6 inches from the broiler; broil until cheese begins to melt.

Guacamole Dip I

 2 ripe avocados, peeled, pitted and mashed
 1 4-ounce container whipped cream cheese
   Seasoned salt

Mix avocado with cream cheese and season to taste. Cover and refrigerate until serving time.

Snow Ice Cream

 ½ cup sugar
 1 cup cold evaporated milk
 1 teaspoon vanilla extract
 1 teaspoon maple extract

Beat above ingredients well with a spoon. Add clean snow, a little at a time, until creamy and the consistency of ice cream.

Party Cookies

Makes 100 cookies.

 ½ cup shortening, softened
 ½ cup butter, softened
 2 cups brown sugar
 2 cups applesauce
 2 eggs, lightly beaten
3½ cups flour
 2 teaspoons baking soda
 1 teaspoon baking powder
 2 teaspoons ground cinnamon
 1 teaspoon ground cloves
 2 teaspoons ground nutmeg
 1 teaspoon salt
 2 cups rolled oats
 2 cups chopped nuts
 1 12-ounce package chocolate chips

Cream first 5 ingredients thoroughly. Sift together flour, baking soda, baking powder, cinnamon, cloves, nutmeg, and salt. Add to creamed mixture. Add remaining ingredients; mix. Drop by teaspoonfuls onto a greased baking sheet. Bake at 375° for 12 to 15 minutes.

Valentine's Day

Valentine Cream Puff Heart

- 1 cup water
- ½ cup butter
- 1 cup sifted flour
- 4 eggs
- 1 10-ounce package frozen strawberries, drained
  Confectioners' sugar

Mark a heart-shaped outline with pencil on a baking sheet. Grease sheet lightly. Bring water and butter to boiling. Reduce heat. Add flour. Stir vigorously over low heat until mixture forms a ball, about 1 minute. Remove from heat. Beat in eggs, one at a time, beating until smooth after each addition. Drop mixture by spoonfuls, with sides touching, onto heart outline on baking sheet. Bake at 400° for 45 minutes. Cool on a rack. Cut off top. Fill shell with cream filling; top with strawberries. Replace top. Dust with confectioners' sugar. Serve at once.

Cream Filling

- 1 3¼-ounce package vanilla pudding
- 1½ cups milk
- 1 cup heavy cream, whipped
- 1 teaspoon vanilla

Combine pudding and milk in a medium saucepan. Cook, stirring constantly, over medium heat until mixture comes to a full rolling boil. Remove from heat. Cover surface of pudding with waxed paper. Cool. Fold in whipped cream and vanilla.

Strawberry Divinity

Makes 2¼ pounds.

- 3 cups sugar
- ¾ cup light corn syrup
- ¾ cup water
- 2 egg whites
- 1 package strawberry-flavored gelatin
- ½ cup flaked coconut
- 1 cup chopped pecans

Combine sugar, corn syrup, and water in a 2-quart saucepan and heat to boiling, stirring constantly. Continue cooking, stirring occasionally, until a small amount of the mixture forms a hard ball when tested in cold water (252° on a candy thermometer). Beat egg whites until foamy, add gelatin, beating until mixture forms peaks. Slowly pour hot syrup into beaten egg whites, beating constantly on high speed of electric mixer. Beat until candy begins to hold its shape. Fold in coconut and nuts; place in a greased 9-inch square pan. Cool and cut into squares.

Pretty Pink Gelatin Salad

- 1 small package mixed fruit-flavored gelatin
- 1 cup boiling water
- 1 cup creamed cottage cheese
- 1 8-ounce can crushed pineapple, drained
- 72 colored miniature marshmallows
- ½ pint whipping cream, whipped

Dissolve gelatin in boiling water. Chill until it thickens. Fold in cottage cheese and pineapple. Allow to thicken. Fold in marshmallows and whipped cream. Fill a 5-cup mold; chill until set.

Split Seconds

- 2 cups sifted flour
- ½ teaspoon baking powder
- ⅔ cup sugar
- ¾ cup butter or margarine, softened
- 1 egg, beaten
- 2 teaspoons vanilla extract
- ⅓ cup red jelly or jam

In a mixing bowl, sift together first 3 ingredients. Blend in butter, egg, and vanilla to form a dough. Place on a lightly floured board. Divide dough into four parts. Shape each into a roll 13 inches long and ¾ inch thick. Place on ungreased baking sheets 4 inches apart and 2 inches from edge of sheet. With a knife handle make a depression ¼ to ⅓ inch deep lengthwise down the center of each. Fill depressions with jelly. Bake at 350° for 15 to 20 minutes until golden brown. While warm, cut diagonally into bars and sprinkle with confectioners' sugar.

Mardi Gras

Mardi Gras Carrot Loaf

Makes 2 loaves.

1¼ cups vegetable oil
2 cups sugar
2 eggs
2 cups grated carrots
1 8-ounce can crushed pineapple and juice
3 cups flour
1 teaspoon baking soda
3 teaspoons ground cinnamon
1 teaspoon salt
2 to 3 teaspoons vanilla extract
1 cup chopped nuts

Blend cooking oil and sugar with eggs. Add carrots and pineapple and juice. Sift dry ingredients; add with vanilla and nuts. Grease and flour 2 loaf pans. Bake at 350° for 1 hour.

Cranberry Cream Cheese Mold

Makes 10 to 12 servings.

1 3-ounce package strawberry-flavored gelatin
1 cup boiling water
1½ cups raw cranberry relish

Dissolve gelatin in boiling water. Cool to room temperature and stir in cranberry relish. Pour into individual molds or 1 large mold. Chill until firm.

Top Layer

1 3-ounce package lemon-flavored gelatin
1½ cups boiling water
2 cups miniature marshmallows
1 cup crushed pineapple
1 3-ounce package cream cheese, softened
½ cup mayonnaise
½ cup whipping cream, whipped

Dissolve lemon gelatin in boiling water. Add marshmallows immediately. Stir until marshmallows dissolve. Add pineapple; chill mixture until partially set. Blend cheese with mayonnaise; stir into second mixture. Fold in whipped cream. Pour onto cranberry layer. Chill. Unmold and serve with salad greens, if desired.

Gourmet Shrimp Cocktail

¼ cup catsup
¼ cup chili sauce
2 teaspoons Worcestershire sauce
4 teaspoons horseradish
1 cup mayonnaise
1 teaspoon salt
½ teaspoon pepper
2 tablespoons chopped chives
¼ cup brandy
2 pounds cooked shrimp

Combine all ingredients except brandy and shrimp. Gradually stir in brandy. Chill in a serving bowl. Arrange the shrimp on a lettuce-lined tray surrounding the bowl of sauce.

Sardine-Stuffed Eggs

6 hard-cooked eggs, cut lengthwise in half
1 4⅜-ounce tin boneless, skinless, oil-packed sardines, drained
¼ cup mayonnaise
2 teaspoons lemon juice
Seasoned salt to taste

Carefully scoop out egg yolks. Mash the yolks and mix well with the other ingredients. Refill the whites. These eggs may be prepared 1 to 2 days in advance, wrapped with plastic wrap, and refrigerated.

Vegetable Ice

1 tablespoon lemon juice
¼ teaspoon Tabasco sauce
6 cups vegetable juice cocktail
Lemon slices, optional
Mint sprigs, optional

Combine ingredients and pour into freezer trays; freeze. Remove from freezer 15 minutes before serving. Spoon into sherbet glasses and garnish with a lemon slice and sprig of mint.

Cheese Puffs

Makes 4 dozen puffs.

- ½ cup butter
- 1 cup boiling water
- 1 cup sifted flour
- ½ teaspoon salt
- 4 eggs
- ½ cup grated Parmesan cheese

Melt butter in water in a saucepan. Add flour and salt all at once. Cook over medium heat, stirring constantly, until mixture leaves the side of the pan. Remove from heat and allow to cool 1 minute. Add eggs, one at a time, beating well until smooth and glossy. Add cheese and mix well. Drop dough by teaspoonfuls onto a greased baking sheet. Bake at 425° for 18 to 20 minutes.

Note: The unbaked dough may be refrigerated, covered, up to 3 days.

Paprika Steak

Makes 6 servings.

- 2 tablespoons flour
- ½ teaspoon paprika
- ¼ teaspoon leaf thyme
- Dash pepper
- 1½ pounds round steak
- 2 tablespoons shortening
- 1 medium onion, sliced
- 1 clove garlic, minced
- 1 10¾-ounce can cream of vegetable soup
- ½ soup can water
- ½ cup sour cream

Combine flour, paprika, thyme, and pepper. Pound into steak with a meat hammer or the edge of a heavy saucer. Cut meat into 6 pieces. Melt the shortening in a skillet; brown meat, onion, and garlic. Blend soup and water; pour over meat. Cover and simmer for 1½ hours, occasionally spooning sauce over meat. Remove meat from pan to heated platter. Stir in sour cream; heat for a few minutes. Pour over meat. Sprinkle with additional paprika.

Double-Quick Dinner Rolls

Makes 1 dozen rolls.

- 1 package dry yeast
- ¾ cup warm water
- ¼ cup sugar
- 1 teaspoon salt
- 2¼ cups flour
- 1 egg
- ¼ cup butter, softened

Dissolve yeast in the warm water. Add sugar, salt, and half of the flour. Beat for 2 minutes. Add egg and butter. Beat with mixer at medium speed until batter is smooth, about 2 minutes. Add the rest of the flour and stir by hand until flour disappears. Scrape sides of bowl. Cover with waxed paper and let stand until double in bulk, about 40 to 50 minutes. Stir down batter in 20 to 25 strokes. Spoon into greased muffin tins, filling half full. Let rise again for about 30 minutes or until batter reaches top of muffin cups. Bake at 425° for 10 to 15 minutes.

Poor Man's Mille-Feuilles

- 1 package graham crackers
- 1 large box vanilla pudding, prepared and cooled
- 1 tablespoon sugar
- 1 teaspoon vanilla extract
- ½ pint whipping cream, whipped

Spread whole graham crackers on the bottom of a 7½ x 10½-inch pan. Cover with a layer of pudding. Add sugar and vanilla to the whipped cream. Spread a layer of whipped cream over pudding layer. Cover with a second layer of whole graham crackers.

Icing

- Milk
- ½ pound confectioners' sugar
- 1 teaspoon vanilla extract
- 1 square baking chocolate, melted

Add enough milk to sugar and vanilla to make a thin frosting. Spread evenly over graham crackers. Drizzle chocolate over icing. Chill 6 hours; serve within 24 hours.

Washington's Birthday

Sour Cherry Cake

Makes 1 8-inch cake.

1¼ cups sugar
½ cup butter, softened
2 eggs
2 cups flour
1 teaspoon baking soda
¼ teaspoon salt
1 teaspoon cinnamon
¾ cup sour milk
1 cup sour cherries

Grease and flour 2 8-inch cake pans. Cream together sugar and butter. Beat in eggs, one at a time. In a separate bowl sift flour, baking soda, salt, and cinnamon. Add butter mixture to flour mixture alternately with milk, beating after each addition. Fold in cherries. Bake at 350° for about 30 minutes.

Sour Cherry Frosting

1 tablespoon butter, softened
1 tablespoon shortening
2½ cups confectioners' sugar
1 teaspoon vanilla extract
Cherry juice

Combine ingredients with enough cherry juice to obtain a spreading consistency. Mix until smooth; frost cake.

Note: To make cherry juice when using fresh sour cherries, cook a small amount of cherries in a little water and sugar to form a syrup. Strain.

Washington Cherry Cheesecake

2 cups graham cracker crumbs
1½ sticks margarine, melted
1¼ cups sugar, divided
2 8-ounce packages cream cheese, softened
2 eggs
1 can cherry pie filling

Combine graham cracker crumbs, margarine, and ¼ cup of the sugar. Line baking pan with crumb mixture; set aside. Beat together cream cheese, remaining 1 cup of sugar, and eggs until smooth and creamy. Pour cheese filling into graham cracker-lined pan; bake at 375° for 15 minutes. Cool. Spread pie filling over top.

Cherries in the Snow

1 small angel food cake
1 1-pound can cherry pie filling
½ pint heavy cream, whipped

Break cake into small pieces. Use half to cover the bottom of a shallow 2-quart glass baking dish. Spread half of the cherry pie filling over cake pieces, smoothing into an even layer with the back of a spoon. Spoon half of the whipped cream over this, smoothing again. Repeat layers, ending with whipped cream. Smooth the cream to cover the entire top of mixture. Cover dish tightly with plastic wrap and refrigerate for 24 hours. Cut into squares.

Bing Cherry Salad

1 cup pitted bing cherries, drain and reserve juice
1 cup crushed pineapple, drain and reserve juice
1 3-ounce package black cherry-flavored gelatin
1 cup chopped pecans or walnuts
1 cup marshmallows, chopped fine

Combine fruit juices and bring to a boil. Add to gelatin; stir until gelatin dissolves. Cool. Stir in fruit, nuts, and marshmallows. Pour into a 5-cup mold. Chill until firm. Unmold onto a lettuce bed and top with cream cheese or salad dressing, if desired.

Fruit Salad Dressing Supreme

2 tablespoons flour
¾ cup sugar
2 eggs, lightly beaten
2 tablespoons butter
2 tablespoons lemon juice
1 cup pineapple juice

Combine all ingredients in the top of a double boiler. Cook, stirring constantly, over boiling water until slightly thickened. Remove from heat and chill. Serve as dressing for fruit salad or gelatin salad.

Sunday Brunch

Orange Blossom Punch

- 1 4-ounce jar maraschino cherries, drained
- 1 8-ounce can pineapple chunks, drained
- 1 24-ounce bottle champagne
- ½ gallon orange juice

Fill a 6-cup ring mold with water. Drop in the cherries and pineapple. Freeze. At serving time pour orange juice and champagne into punch bowl. Unmold ice ring by dipping into 2 inches hot water; slide ice ring into punch.

Salmon Ball

- 1 16-ounce can red salmon, drained, remove skin and bones
- 1 8-ounce package cream cheese, softened
- 1 small onion, minced
- 2 tablespoons lemon juice
- ½ cup minced parsley
- ¼ cup chopped nuts

Flake salmon into a bowl. Add cream cheese; blend well. Add onion and lemon juice. Mix well. Shape into a ball and wrap in waxed paper; refrigerate until firm. Sprinkle parsley and nuts on waxed paper; mix well. Roll salmon ball in mixture until coated. Refrigerate until serving time. Place in center of platter and surround with crackers to serve.

Cheese and Egg Brunch

Makes 8 servings.

- 6 slices bread, cubed
- 1 large can mushrooms
- ½ cup sliced, stuffed olives
- ¾ cup grated sharp Cheddar cheese
- ¾ cup grated Swiss cheese
- 4 eggs, beaten
- 2 cups milk
- ½ teaspoon dry mustard
- ½ teaspoon salt

Place half of the bread cubes in a buttered 3-quart casserole. Layer with the mushrooms, olives, and cheeses. Top with the remaining bread cubes. Combine eggs, milk, mustard and salt; pour over all. Refrigerate overnight. Bake, uncovered, at 350° for 1 hour. Let stand 10 minutes before serving. Serve with sausage or bacon, hot rolls or sweet rolls.

Baked Canadian Bacon

- 3 pounds Canadian bacon
- 1 orange, cut into thin slices
  Whole cloves
- ½ cup molasses
- ¼ cup water
- ½ cup orange juice
- ¼ cup sugar
- ¼ teaspoon dry mustard

Remove casing from bacon and place, fat-side up, in an open pan. Bake at 325° for 2 hours. Remove from the oven and attach orange slices to bacon with cloves. Mix remaining ingredients. Pour over bacon and bake, basting often, at 325° for 30 minutes.

Fruit Medley

- 1 cup cubed cantaloupe
- 1 cup raspberries
- 1 cup pineapple chunks
- ½ cup sugar syrup

Combine fruits in a large bowl. Mix lightly. Pour sugar syrup over fruit mixture. Chill 30 minutes.

Sugar Syrup

- ½ cup sugar
- 1 cup water

Combine sugar and water. Boil 5 minutes. Cool.

Blueberry Muffins

- ½ cup sour milk
- 1 teaspoon baking soda
- 1 cup brown sugar
- ½ cup shortening
- 2 eggs
- ½ teaspoon salt
- 2½ cups sifted flour, divided
- 1 pint blueberries

Combine sour milk and baking soda; stir until baking soda dissolves; set aside. Cream sugar and shortening. Add eggs, 1 at a time. Combine salt and 2 cups of the flour. Alternately add sour milk and flour to sugar mixture. Mix the ½ cup flour and blueberries; fold into batter. Pour into greased muffin tins. Bake at 350° for approximately 25 minutes until light brown.

Special Luncheon

Claret Cup

Makes 8 to 10 servings.

- 1 quart claret wine
- 1 ounce Maraschino liqueur
- 2 ounces curacao liqueur
- 2 tablespoons granulated sugar

Combine all the ingredients in a pitcher. Serve over ice in tall glasses. Garnish each glass with a long toothpick skewered with a slice of orange, a chunk of pineapple, and a sprig of fresh mint, if desired.

Refrigerator Rolls

- 1 package dry yeast
- 1 cup warm water (110 to 115°)
- 1 tablespoon salt
- 2 tablespoons (heaping) shortening
- ½ cup sugar
- 2 cups boiling water
- 8 cups flour
- 3 eggs, beaten

Dissolve yeast in warm water; set aside. Combine salt, shortening, and sugar in a large bowl. Stir in boiling water. Cool to warm. Add enough flour to slightly thicken. Add yeast mixture; beat well. Add the eggs and remainder of the flour. Knead dough until smooth. Let rise until double in bulk. Punch down and place in a well-greased bowl. Cover and refrigerate. When ready to use, cut off desired amount of dough, shape and let rise about 3 hours. Bake at 375° for 20 minutes. Punch down any remaining dough and refrigerate until needed.

Lemoned Carrots

- 1 1-pound can diced carrots, reserve ¼ cup liquid
- 1 teaspoon sugar
- 1 teaspoon lemon juice
- 2 teaspoons butter
- ½ teaspoon grated lemon peel

Combine all ingredients including carrot liquid and heat. Sprinkle on lemon peel.

Imperial Crab

Makes 4 servings.

- ¼ cup butter
- 1 cup half and half
- 1 teaspoon dry mustard
- 1 teaspoon lemon juice
- 2 teaspoons Worcestershire sauce
- 1 teaspoon salt
- ¾ teaspoon pepper
- 1 egg, lightly beaten
- 1 pound crabmeat
- Cracker crumbs

Melt butter in a double boiler. Mix in half and half, mustard, lemon juice, Worcestershire sauce, salt, pepper, and egg, stirring constantly. Add crabmeat. Fill individual casseroles with mixture. Sprinkle on cracker crumbs. Bake at 400° for 30 minutes until golden brown.

Strawberry Dream

Makes 12 to 14 servings.

- 1 cup butter
- ½ cup brown sugar
- 2 cups flour
- 1 cup chopped nuts

Combine ingredients and place in a 9 x 13-inch pan. Bake at 400° for 15 minutes, stirring occasionally. When brown press half of the mixture into an oblong pan. Spread on Filling; top with remaining crumb mixture. Freeze overnight until ready to use.

Filling

- 1 10-ounce package frozen strawberries, thawed
- 2 egg whites
- 1 cup sugar
- 1 tablespoon lemon juice
- 1 teaspoon vanilla extract
- ½ pint whipping cream, whipped

Place all ingredients, except whipped cream, in a large mixing bowl. Beat with an electric mixer for 20 minutes. Fold in the whipped cream.

"May the roads rise with you, And the wind be always at your back; And may the Lord hold you in the hollow of His hand."

OLD GAELIC BLESSING

St. Patrick's Day

Emerald Salad

Makes 8 to 10 servings.

- 1 16-ounce can sliced peaches, drained, reserve syrup
- 2 3-ounce packages lime-flavored gelatin
- 2 cups boiling water
- 1 cup cold water
- 1 red maraschino cherry
- 1 cup grapes, halved and seeded (or 1 8¾-ounce can grapes, drained)
  Lettuce
  Cottage cheese

Add enough water to syrup to make 1 cup. Dissolve gelatin in the boiling water. Add the 1 cup water and the peach syrup. Chill until partially set. Place 1 cup of gelatin mixture in a 6-cup mold. Press 12 peach slices into gelatin, forming a sunburst. Place cherry in center. Dice remaining peaches. Add peaches and grapes to remaining gelatin. Pour into mold; chill until firm. Unmold onto chilled serving plate. Surround with lettuce cups filled with cottage cheese.

Shamrock Rolls

Refrigerater Rolls dough (Recipe on page 13)

Shape the dough into small balls; brush with melted butter. Arrange 4 balls in each cup of a greased muffin tin. Allow dough to rise and bake according to recipe directions.

Scalloped Tomatoes

Makes 4 servings.

- 6 medium tomatoes, peeled and quartered
- ¾ cup water
- 2 slices toast, buttered and cubed
- 8 soda crackers, broken
- 1 teaspoon butter
- ½ teaspoon dried parsley
  Salt and pepper to taste

Cook tomatoes in the water until mushy. Add buttered toast and 6 of the broken soda crackers. Add butter and parsley; salt and pepper to taste. Before serving, top with remaining crackers.

Corned Beef and Cabbage

- 1 4-pound corned beef brisket
- 1 head cabbage

Wash brisket; place in a kettle and cover with cold water. Bring water to a boil; cover and simmer 30 minutes. Drain. Cover with fresh boiling water and simmer until meat is tender. Chop cabbage into wedges. About 20 minutes before meat is done, add cabbage. Cook uncovered for 10 to 15 minutes. Do not overcook the cabbage.

Irish Bread

- 4 cups flour
- 4 teaspoons baking powder
- ¼ teaspoon baking soda
- ½ tablespoon salt
- 2 tablespoons shortening
- 1 tablespoon butter
- 2 eggs, lightly beaten
  Buttermilk
  Raisins, citron or currants, optional

Mix dry ingredients. Cut in shortening and butter until mixture is crumbly. Add eggs and buttermilk. Add raisins, citron, or currants as desired. Bake at 350° about 1 hour.

Pistachio Cake

- 1 16-ounce box almond-flavored cake mix (or use white cake mix and 1 teaspoon almond extract)
- 1 3-ounce package pistachio instant pudding
  Green food coloring, optional
- ¾ cup cold water
- ¾ cup vegetable oil
- 1 teaspoon almond extract, optional
- 4 eggs

Blend cake mix and pudding. If more color is desired, add a few drops of green food coloring to the water. Add water and oil to the cake mixture. Add extract and eggs, one at a time, using low speed of mixer. Beat 5 minutes. Oil a large angel food cake or bundt pan. Bake at 350° for 45 to 50 minutes. Cool before removing from pan.

Note: This cake freezes well.

Springtime Favorites

Springtime Avocado Salad

- 1 avocado, sliced
- 1 can mandarin oranges, drained
- ¼ cup chopped red onion
- ½ cup Creamy French Dressing

Combine fruits and the onion. Add dressing. Refrigerate to mix flavors.

Creamy French Dressing

- ¾ cup sugar
- 1 teaspoon salt
- 1 teaspoon dry mustard
- ½ teaspoon paprika
  Dash pepper
- 2 egg yolks, well beaten
- ½ cup vinegar
- 2 cups salad oil
- ¼ cup boiling water

Combine dry ingredients. Add to egg yolks. Blend in vinegar alternately with small amounts of oil. Stir in water. Store in refrigerator.

Blender Instructions: Beat egg yolks; add dry ingredients, vinegar, and oil. Blend well. Pour in boiling water.

Pork Croquettes

Makes 4 servings.

- 2 tablespoons flour
- 2 tablespoons butter or margarine
  Pinch salt
- 1 cup milk
- 2 cups ground cooked pork
- 1 egg, lightly beaten
  Cracker crumbs

Blend first 3 ingredients in a saucepan; add milk. Stir over low heat until thick. Stir in pork. When cool enough to handle, shape mixture into cylinders. Chill in refrigerator for several hours or overnight. Dip in egg and crumbs; deep fry until golden.

Note: May be served with a white sauce. If desired, shape into flat, round patties and fry in skillet.

Lettuce and Dandelion Salad

- 2 cups fresh dandelion greens, washed
- ½ head lettuce, torn into bite-size pieces
- 1 cup thinly sliced onion
  French dressing
- 1 hard-cooked egg, sliced
  Grated Parmesan cheese
  Paprika

Rinse dandelion greens in ice water to crisp. Drain well on paper towels. Place lettuce, dandelion greens and onion slices in a garlic-rubbed salad bowl. Pour French dressing over all. Toss lightly until ingredients are coated. Garnish with egg slices, grated cheese and paprika.

Dill Dip

- 1 cup mayonnaise
- 1 cup sour cream
- 1 teaspoon seasoned salt
- 1 tablespoon chopped parsley
- 1 tablespoon dillweed
- 1 tablespoon dry onion flakes
  Lemon juice to taste

Combine all ingredients; chill. Serve with raw vegetables.

Surprise Coconut Pie

Makes 2 9-inch pies.

- 4 eggs
- 1¾ cups sugar
- 2 cups milk
- 1 teaspoon vanilla
- ½ cup flour
- ¼ cup margarine, melted
- 1 7-ounce package flaked coconut

In a large mixing bowl, beat together eggs, sugar, milk, vanilla, flour, and margarine until well combined and fold in the coconut. Pour into 2 greased and floured 9-inch pie pans. Bake in a preheated 350° oven for 40 minutes or until golden brown. Crust forms as pie bakes.

Ham-Asparagus Rolls au Gratin

Makes 8 rolls.

    3 tablespoons butter or margarine
    3 tablespoons flour
    ¾ teaspoon salt
    2 cups milk
    1 cup shredded pasteurized process Swiss cheese
    1⅓ cups cooked rice
    8 ¼-inch slices cooked ham
    24 to 32 slender asparagus spears, cooked
       and drained
    ¼ cup shredded Parmesan cheese

Melt butter in a saucepan. Blend in flour and salt. Add milk and cook, stirring constantly, until thick. Add cheese and stir until melted. Blend 1 cup sauce into rice. Spoon an equal amount of rice mixture onto end of ham slice. Top each slice with 3 or 4 asparagus spears and roll ham around filling. Arrange rolls in shallow 2-quart baking dish. Pour remaining sauce over rolls. Sprinkle with Parmesan cheese. Bake at 350° until hot, about 25 to 30 minutes.

Crab Louis

Makes 6 servings.

    1 head lettuce, torn into bite-size pieces
    1 cup crabmeat, more if desired
    2 avocados
    1 small can julienned beets, drained
    1 small can pitted olives, drained
    2 hard-cooked eggs
    2 tomatoes
    ½ cup sliced green onion
    ½ green pepper, sliced

Place lettuce on serving plates. Arrange remaining ingredients on lettuce. Pour Louis Dressing over all.

Louis Dressing

    ¼ cup chili sauce
    ½ pound sour cream
    ¼ cup minced green pepper
    ¼ cup minced green onion
    1 cup mayonnaise
    1 teaspoon lemon juice
      Salt to taste

Blend all ingredients thoroughly.

Lima Beans in Sour Cream

    1 pound baby lima beans
    3 teaspoons salt
    ½ cup butter, softened
    ¾ cup brown sugar
    1 tablespoon dry mustard
    1 tablespoon molasses
    1 cup sour cream

Cook lima beans until tender; rinse with hot water. Place in a large casserole dish. Combine remaining ingredients and stir into beans. Bake at 350° for 1 hour.

Frozen Strawberry Jam

    4 cups sugar
    2 cups strawberries, crushed
    ¾ cup water
    1 box pectin

Add sugar to fruit; mix well. Combine water and pectin in a saucepan. Bring to a boil; boil 1 minute, stirring constantly. Stir into fruit mixture. Continue stirring 3 minutes. A few sugar crystals will remain. Quickly ladle into jars; cover at once with tight lids (no paraffin is necessary). Set at room temperature 24 hours. Store in the freezer. Jam is ready to eat after 3 weeks.

Rhubarb Cake

Makes 12 servings.

    1½ cups brown sugar
    ½ cup shortening, softened
    1 egg
    1 cup sour milk or buttermilk
    2 cups flour
    1 teaspoon baking soda
    1 teaspoon vanilla extract
    1½ to 2 cups chopped rhubarb
    ½ cup sugar
    1 teaspoon ground cinnamon

Cream together the brown sugar and shortening. Add the egg, sour milk, flour, soda, vanilla, and rhubarb. Stir to blend all ingredients. Place in a 9 x 13-inch greased and floured pan. Mix sugar and cinnamon; sprinkle over top. Bake at 350° for 35 minutes.

Easter

Champagne and Strawberries

1 pint fresh strawberries, washed and hulled
1 bottle champagne or sparkling Burgundy

Divide berries among champagne or sherbet glasses. Pour chilled champagne over berries.

Melon Ball Treat

Watermelon
Cantaloupe
Honeydew melon

Scoop out melon balls. Place in fruit cups. Garnish with lime wedges, if desired.

Party Avocado Salad

1 avocado, cubed
1 medium tomato, cut up
1 small onion, minced
1 teaspoon lemon juice
Salt and pepper to taste
Mayonnaise

Mix all ingredients with enough mayonnaise to moisten.

Fresh Vegetable Casserole

1½ pounds mushrooms, sliced or ¾ pound
mushrooms and ¾ pound carrots
1 onion, sliced
1 tomato, sliced
1 tablespoon butter
1 tablespoon flour
½ cup sour cream
Juice of ½ lemon
1½ ounces brandy
½ teaspoon salt
⅛ teaspoon pepper
1 tablespoon chopped parsley

Layer vegetables in a 2-quart casserole dish. Make a white sauce with the butter, flour and sour cream. Add lemon juice and brandy to the sour cream mixture. Pour over vegetables. Add salt and pepper. Sprinkle parsley over all. Cover. Bake at 350° for 45 minutes.

Stuffed Leg of Lamb

1 5- to 6-pound leg of lamb
½ pound ground raw veal
½ pound ground cooked lean ham
½ pound dry bread crumbs
½ pound fresh mushrooms, minced
1 egg
1 small clove garlic, crushed
1 tablespoon Worcestershire sauce
1 tablespoon orange marmalade with rind
Salt, pepper, oregano to taste

Bone lamb, leaving 3 inches of shank bone. Preheat oven to 325°. Mix remaining ingredients until smooth and compact. Pack into cavity of lamb. Sew opening securely with heavy string. Place lamb, fat side up, on a rack in a roasting pan. Roast for 30 to 35 minutes per pound. Serve with mint jelly or spiced peaches.

Ice Cream Parfait

Fill parfait glasses with alternate layers of mint ice cream and cold fudge sauce. Top with whipped cream and a sprig of mint. This can be frozen.

Coconut Cookies

1 cup shortening
1 cup brown sugar
2 eggs
1 teaspoon vanilla extract
2½ cups flour
1 teaspoon baking soda
½ teaspoon baking powder
½ teaspoon salt
2 cups bran flakes
2 cups coconut

Cream shortening, sugar, and eggs; add vanilla. Sift flour, baking soda, baking powder, and salt together. Put bran flakes and coconut in a bowl. Mix well with flour mixture, add liquid mixture and mix to soft dough. Form into small balls; flatten on a baking sheet about 2 inches apart. Bake at 400° until done.

Hot Cross Buns

- 1 package dry yeast
- 2 tablespoons warm water (110 to 115°)
- 1 cup scalded milk
- ¼ cup sugar
- 1½ teaspoons salt
- ½ teaspoon ground cinnamon
- ¾ cup currants
- 2 eggs, well beaten
- 4 cups sifted flour
- ½ cup butter, melted

Soften yeast in the warm water. In a separate bowl, combine the scalded milk, sugar, salt, cinnamon, and currants. Cool to lukewarm. Add yeast mixture and eggs. Add 2 cups of the flour and mix. Add the melted butter and beat well. Add remaining flour gradually. Mix but do not knead. Place dough in a greased bowl, turning to grease top of dough. Cover and chill until firm enough to handle. Divide dough into 18 to 20 portions and shape into buns. Set aside until double in bulk. Place on greased baking sheet. Bake at 400° for 10 to 15 minutes. Using the Frosting form a cross on each bun.

Frosting

- 3 cups sifted confectioners' sugar
- 3 tablespoons butter, melted
- 3 tablespoons milk
- 1 tablespoon vanilla extract

Combine all ingredients; mix until smooth.

Apple Rolls

Makes 12 servings.

- 2 cups flour
- 4 teaspoons baking powder
- ¼ teaspoon salt
- 6 tablespoons shortening
- ¾ cup milk
- 6 to 8 apples, peeled and diced
  Ground cinnamon
- ¼ cup sugar
- 1½ cups sugar
- 2 cups water

Mix the flour, baking powder, and salt. Cut in shortening with pastry cutter. Add milk and mix until mixture resembles coarse crumbs. Roll out about ¼ inch thick on a floured board. Spread apples over dough. Sprinkle with cinnamon and the ¼ cup sugar. Roll up as for a jelly roll. Cut into 12 slices. Place in a 9 x 13-inch pan. Boil the 1½ cups sugar and 2 cups water. Pour over apple rolls. Bake at 375° until brown. Serve with whipped cream.

Easter Egg Bread

- 5 eggs
- 1 cup flour
- ¼ cup sugar
- 1 teaspoon salt
- 1 package dry yeast
- ⅔ cup milk
- 2 tablespoons butter
- 2 eggs
- 1¼ to 2 cups flour

Dip the 5 uncooked eggs in food coloring to dye shells. In a large bowl, thoroughly mix next 4 ingredients. Combine milk and butter in a saucepan. Heat until warm, not melted. Gradually add to dry ingredients; beat 2 minutes at medium speed with an electric mixer. Add the 2 eggs and ½ cup of the flour. Beat 2 minutes at high speed. Stir in remaining ¾ to 1½ cups flour to make a soft dough. Turn out onto a lightly floured board. Knead 8 to 10 minutes until smooth and elastic. Place in a greased bowl, turning to grease top. Allow to rise in a warm place, covered, until double in bulk, about 1 hour. Punch down dough. Divide dough into 2 equal balls. Let stand, covered, for 10 minutes. Roll each ball into a long roll about 36 inches long and 1 to 1½ inches thick. Using the 2 long pieces of dough, form a loosely braided ring, leaving spaces for the 5 colored eggs. Place on a buttered 15½ x 12-inch baking sheet. Place colored eggs into spaces in the braid. Cover loosely with a towel. Set dough aside in a warm place until double in bulk. Brush bread with melted butter and sprinkle with tiny multicolored decorations. Bake at 350° for 50 to 55 minutes.

Tossed Green Salad

Select several varieties of fresh, crisp greens. In addition to lettuce (romaine, bibb, iceberg, or Boston), try spinach, mustard greens, watercress, curly endive, or chicory. Wash and drain the greens thoroughly. Tear into bite-size pieces, place in a salad bowl and chill in the refrigerator several hours. Toss with dressing just before serving. Top with croutons, bacon bits, anchovies, crumbled cheese, minced chives, or whatever you prefer.

Onion Dressing

    1 medium onion, grated
1¾ cups sugar
    1 teaspoon celery seed
    2 teaspoons salt
    1 teaspoon dry mustard
 ¾ cup cider vinegar
    1 pint salad oil

Mix first 5 ingredients together. Slowly stir in vinegar and salad oil alternately.

Ham de Mullich

    1 thick center cut ham slice
      Mustard and red pepper to taste
    1 onion, sliced
    1 cup water
    2 potatoes, peeled, quartered and parboiled

Sear ham on both sides in a hot skillet. Place in a shallow roasting pan. Spread with mustard; sprinkle on red pepper. Add onion on top of ham; pour in water. Cover and bake at 350° for 30 minutes. Add potatoes and bake until slightly brown, adding more water if necessary.

Baked Pineapple

2½ cups crushed pineapple
 ½ cup sugar
 ¼ pound butter or margarine, melted
    4 eggs, beaten
    5 slices bread, torn into small pieces

Combine all ingredients in a baking dish. Bake at 350° for 45 minutes.

Note: This is good served with ham or lamb.

Spiced Orange Pot Roast

Makes 6 to 8 servings.

    4 to 5 pounds beef chuck roast
    1 tablespoon shortening or bacon drippings
 ½ cup minced onion
    1 clove garlic, minced
    1 8-ounce can tomato sauce
    2 cups orange sections
    2 tablespoons sugar
    1 tablespoon grated orange rind
1½ teaspoons salt
 ½ teaspoon ground nutmeg
 ½ teaspoon ground cinnamon
 ¼ teaspoon ground cloves
      Dash pepper
      Orange slices, optional
      Watercress or parsley, optional

Brown meat slowly on both sides in hot shortening. Add onion and garlic. Cover and cook 20 minutes. Pour tomato sauce, orange sections, sugar, and grated orange rind over meat. Sprinkle with salt and spices. Cover and cook slowly until meat is tender, about 2 hours. Garnish with orange slices and watercress or parsley, if desired.

Baked Corn

    1 16-ounce can cream-style corn
    1 cup milk
    1 egg, well beaten
 ¾ teaspoon salt and pepper
    1 cup cracker crumbs
 ½ cup buttered cracker crumbs

Heat corn and milk. Gradually stir in egg. Add seasonings and 1 cup cracker crumbs. Place in a buttered baking dish. Sprinkle buttered crumbs on top. Bake at 350° for 1 hour.

Creamy Uncooked Cherry Pie

    1 medium can cherry pie filling
    1 prepared graham cracker piecrust
    2 cups (heaping) whipped cream
 ½ cup finely chopped pecans

Pour cherry pie filling onto piecrust. Spread with whipped cream. Sprinkle on nuts. Chill 2 hours. Serve.

Mother's Day

French Silk Chocolate Pie

    ¾ cup butter, softened
    1 cup sugar
    3 eggs, beaten
    2 ounces chocolate, melted
    1 teaspoon vanilla extract
    1 9-inch pie shell, baked

Cream butter thoroughly; add sugar, mixing well. Add eggs and blend. Add cooled chocolate; beat until smooth. Add vanilla and pour into pie shell. Top with whipped cream and nuts, if desired.

Whipped Cream Substitute

    ½ cup flour
    2 cups milk
    1 pound butter or margarine, softened
    2 cups sugar
    2 teaspoons vanilla extract

Cook flour and milk until thick; cool. Cream butter, sugar and vanilla until fluffy. Beat in cooled flour mixture.

Forgotten Cookies

Makes 2 dozen.

    2 egg whites, room temperature
    ⅔ cup sugar
      Pinch salt
    1 teaspoon vanilla extract
    1 cup chopped pecans
    1 cup chocolate bits or cornflakes or crisp rice cereal
    1 cup coconut, optional

Beat egg whites until foamy. Gradually add sugar; continue beating until stiff. Add salt and vanilla; mix well. Add pecans and remaining ingredients. Preheat oven to 350°. Drop cookies by the spoonful on ungreased foil-covered baking sheets. Place cookies in oven and immediately turn off oven. Leave cookies in closed oven overnight. Do not open oven door until the end of baking time.

Bran Muffins

    1 cup boiling water
    3 cups all-bran cereal
    ½ cup vegetable shortening, softened
    1½ cups white sugar
    2 eggs, beaten
    2 cups buttermilk
    2½ cups flour
    2½ teaspoons baking soda
    ¼ teaspoon salt
    ⅓ cup currants, optional

Pour the boiling water over the bran cereal. Set aside. Cream shortening and sugar. Add beaten eggs and buttermilk. Sift flour, soda, and salt together. Add to shortening mixture. Fold in bran. Add currants, if desired. Do not stir or beat. Spoon gently into greased muffin tins. Bake at 400° for 15 to 18 minutes.

Note: This muffin batter will keep in the refrigerator for 6 weeks.

Yummy Cake

    1 package yellow cake mix
    1 package pineapple or vanilla instant pudding
    ¾ cup vegetable oil
    4 eggs, well beaten
    10 ounces lemon-lime soda

Combine all ingredients except soda; add soda and beat well. Bake in a 13 x 9-inch greased and floured pan at 350° for 40 minutes. Pour Icing over cake while still hot.

Icing

    3 eggs, beaten
    1½ cups sugar
    2 tablespoons flour
    ½ cup margarine
    1 cup crushed pineapple, drained
    1 small can coconut

Combine eggs, sugar, flour, and margarine in a saucepan. Cook over medium heat until thick. Add pineapple and coconut.

Father's Day

Curried Fruit

3½ cups canned peach halves, drained
3½ cups canned pear halves, drained
3½ cups canned pineapple chunks, drained
⅓ cup butter or margarine, melted
½ cup light brown sugar
½ teaspoon curry powder
    Maraschino cherries

Arrange fruits in baking dish. Mix butter, sugar, and curry powder; spoon over fruit. Bake, uncovered, at 350° for 1 hour. Refrigerate at least 24 hours. Add a maraschino cherry to each peach and pear half. Heat at 350° for 30 to 40 minutes. Serve warm.

Clear Mushroom Soup

Makes 4 servings.

1 pound mushrooms
4 cups consommé
4 teaspoons sherry

Chop mushrooms. Add to consommé and simmer, tightly covered, for 30 minutes. Strain and reheat. Add sherry.

Sweet Potato Souffle'

2 cups cooked or canned, mashed sweet potatoes
1¼ cups granulated sugar
6 tablespoons butter or margarine
1 cup milk (if canned potatoes are used, use only ½ cup milk)
½ teaspoon ground nutmeg
½ teaspoon ground cinnamon

Mix all ingredients. Pour into casserole and bake at 400° for 20 minutes. Cover with Topping. Bake for 10 minutes.

Topping

¾ cup crushed cornflakes
½ cup pecans, chopped
½ cup brown sugar
6 tablespoons butter, melted

Combine all ingredients; mix well.

Sweet and Sour Spareribs

Makes 4 servings.

2 pounds spareribs
2 small cloves garlic, minced
¼ cup brown sugar
¼ cup soy sauce
2 tablespoons vinegar
2 cups canned pineapple chunks, reserve juice
2 tablespoons cornstarch

Cut spareribs in 1½-inch pieces. Combine all ingredients except pineapple and cornstarch. Simmer 1 hour. Set aside for a few minutes. Pour off excess fat. Place meat in a separate bowl. Heat liquid. Add pineapple juice to liquid; bring to a boil. Add cornstarch; cook until thick. Pour sauce over spareribs. Arrange pineapple chunks on top. Serve hot.

Hash-Brown Potatoes

2 tablespoons shortening
6 potatoes, grated
1 onion, minced
1 egg, lightly beaten
    Salt and pepper to taste

Melt shortening in a skillet. Mix all other ingredients together; spread evenly in skillet. Sauté until golden. Turn and brown other side. Cut into wedges and serve immediately.

Broccoli Casserole

⅓ cup margarine, melted
1 teaspoon salt
1 cup grated sharp cheese
1 egg, beaten
1 cup milk
1 small onion, diced
1 cup cooked rice
1 10-ounce package frozen chopped broccoli, cooked and drained

Combine margarine, salt, cheese, egg, milk, and onion. Blend with rice. Add broccoli. Pour into buttered casserole and bake at 350° for 1 hour.

Tomato Casserole

8 slices bread
½ pound Velveeta cheese, sliced
1 16-ounce can stewed tomatoes
2 eggs, beaten
1 cup milk
½ teaspoon salt
Pepper to taste

Place bread slices in buttered baking dish. Top with thin slices of cheese. Cover with layer of tomatoes. Repeat three times. Beat eggs; add milk, salt, and pepper. Pour into baking dish and bake at 325° for 30 minutes.

Banana Nut Bread

Makes 2 loaves.

1 cup sugar
½ cup margarine, softened
2 eggs, beaten
3 bananas, mashed
3 cups flour
1 teaspoon baking soda
1 teaspoon vanilla extract
1 cup chopped walnuts

Cream sugar and margarine; add eggs and bananas. Combine and stir in remaining ingredients. Place in greased bread pans and bake at 325° for 45 minutes.

Note: This bread freezes well.

Crown-of-Gold Meat Loaf

Makes 6 to 8 servings.

1½ cups fine, soft bread crumbs
1½ pounds lean ground beef
4 egg yolks
1½ teaspoons salt
1½ tablespoons prepared horseradish
2 tablespoons minced onion
2 tablespoons prepared mustard
3 tablespoons minced green pepper
⅓ cup catsup

Mix bread crumbs with meat. Combine remaining ingredients; blend into meat-bread mixture. Pack lightly into a 9-inch casserole and bake at 325° for 30 minutes. Remove from oven and cover with Topping. Return to oven and bake 20 to 25 minutes longer or until tipped with brown.

Topping

4 egg whites
¼ teaspoon cream of tartar
¼ cup prepared mustard

Beat egg whites until foamy; add cream of tartar and beat until very stiff. Gently fold in the mustard.

Golden Sugar Cookies

2½ cups sifted flour
1 teaspoon baking soda
1 teaspoon cream of tartar
¼ teaspoon salt
1 cup butter, softened
1 teaspoon vanilla extract
½ teaspoon lemon extract
2 cups sugar
3 egg yolks

Sift together flour, soda, cream of tartar, and salt; set aside. Cream butter and extracts until smooth. Gradually add sugar, creaming until fluffy. Add egg yolks one at a time, beating well after each addition. Add dry ingredients slowly to the creamed mixture. Beat until blended. Form dough into 1-inch balls and place 2 inches apart on an ungreased baking sheet. Bake at 350° for 10 minutes or until golden brown.

Sour Milk Chocolate Cake

Makes 1 8-inch cake.

5 teaspoons cocoa
1 cup sugar
Pinch salt
½ cup shortening, softened
1 teaspoon baking soda
1 cup sour milk
2 cups flour
1 teaspoon vanilla extract

Mix cocoa with water to make a paste. Cream sugar, salt, and shortening. Add baking soda to milk in a small bowl. Add to shortening mixture; add flour, then vanilla and cocoa paste. Bake at 350° for 30 to 35 minutes.

Vegetable Dippers

Use the following relishes with a favorite dip:

Radishes
Celery hearts
Cucumber petals
Carrot crinkles
Cauliflowerets
Green onions
Broccoli buds
Cherry tomatoes

Guacamole Dip II

Makes 1 cup.

1 cup mashed avocado
1 tablespoon lemon juice
1 teaspoon salt
1½ teaspoons grated lemon

Combine all ingredients and mix well. Chill several hours. Serve with chips or crackers.

Note: For variety, add 1 or more of the following:

Dash Tabasco sauce
1 teaspoon curry powder
1 teaspoon Worcestershire sauce
½ teaspoon chili powder

Shrimp de Jonghe

Makes 8 servings.

1 cup butter, melted
2 cloves garlic, minced
⅓ cup chopped parsley
½ teaspoon paprika
Dash cayenne pepper
2 hard-cooked eggs, whites and yolks separated
⅔ cup cooking sherry
2 cups soft bread crumbs
5 to 6 cups cleaned, cooked shrimp
Chopped parsley

Mix butter, garlic, parsley, paprika, pepper, finely chopped egg white, and sherry. Add the bread crumbs and toss. Place shrimp in an 11 x 7 x 1½-inch baking dish. Spoon butter mixture over top. Bake at 325° for 25 minutes. Garnish with parsley and grated egg yolks.

Sweet and Sour Dressing

1 onion, chopped
½ cup vinegar
1 teaspoon salt
1 teaspoon dry mustard
1 teaspoon celery salt
1 cup sugar
1 cup salad oil

Place all ingredients, except oil, in a blender. Blend until onion is liquid. Add oil and beat again. Serve on lettuce or tossed salad.

Scalloped Corn

1 16-ounce can cream-style corn
1 cup milk
1 cup cracker crumbs
2 eggs, lightly beaten
Salt and pepper to taste

Mix all ingredients together. Spoon into a buttered 1½-quart casserole. Dot with butter. Bake at 350° for 45 minutes.

Pineapple Angel Dessert

Makes 15 servings.

1 cup cold water
1 cup boiling water
1 cup pineapple juice
2 envelopes unflavored gelatin
4 packages whipped topping
1 cup sugar
2 cups crushed pineapple, drained
1 large angel food cake
Coconut
Maraschino cherries

Add cold water, boiling water, and pineapple juice to the unflavored gelatin, mixing well. Allow to thicken. Combine 2 packages prepared whipped topping, sugar, and crushed pineapple. Fold into the gelatin mixture. Break the angel food cake into small pieces; line the bottom of a 9 x 13-inch baking pan with the pieces. Add a layer of pineapple mixture. Repeat with remaining cake and pineapple mixture. Prepare remaining 2 packages of the whipped topping. Spread over top, sprinkle with coconut and dot with maraschino cherries. Chill 3 hours.

New Homemaker

Fun Dip

2 cups sour cream
1 teaspoon salt
1 teaspoon Worcestershire sauce
4 drops Tabasco sauce
¼ teaspoon dry mustard
1 teaspoon dry dillweed
2 tablespoons minced pimiento, rinsed and drained

Combine all ingredients and refrigerate 2 hours to blend flavors. Serve with crisp vegetables such as whole radishes, cauliflower and broccoli flowerets, raw zucchini strips, and cherry tomatoes.

Speedy Rolls

2 cups warm water (110 to 115°)
⅓ cup sugar
2 packages dry yeast
1 tablespoon salt
6½ cups sifted flour
2 eggs
⅓ cup shortening, softened

Place warm water, sugar, and yeast in a mixing bowl. Add salt and 2 cups of the flour. Beat 2 minutes. Add eggs and shortening. Beat 1 minute. Gradually add remaining flour. Stir until dough is formed. Allow dough to stand in bowl for 20 minutes for easy handling. Form dough into balls; place on a greased baking sheet. Bake at 350° for 25 to 30 minutes until done.

Note: The dough may be refrigerated for 1 or 2 days.

Five-Can Casserole

Makes 6 servings.

1 10¾-ounce can mushroom soup
1 10¾-ounce can chicken with rice soup
1 small can evaporated milk
1 can chow mein noodles
1 can chicken, or 1 cup diced cooked chicken

Mix all ingredients together, place in casserole and top with crushed potato chips. Bake at 350° for 1 hour.

Oven Beef Stew

2 pounds beef stew meat
6 carrots, diced
3 medium potatoes, diced
3 ribs celery, diced
1 large onion, diced
1 teaspoon salt
1 tablespoon sugar
2 tablespoons tapioca
½ cup tomato sauce

Mix all ingredients. Spoon into a roaster pan and cover tightly. Bake at 250° for 4 hours. Do not remove cover during baking time.

Mushroom Scalloped Potatoes

1 10¾-ounce can cream of mushroom soup
½ cup grated American cheese
¼ cup minced onion
1 teaspoon salt
⅔ cup evaporated milk
4 cups sliced potatoes
¼ cup grated American cheese

Combine soup, the ½ cup cheese, onion, salt, and milk. Add potatoes. Mix and put in a greased baking dish. Top with the ¼ cup cheese. Bake at 375° until potatoes are tender, about 1 hour and 15 minutes.

Super Baking Powder Biscuits

2 cups flour
½ teaspoon salt
4 teaspoons baking powder
½ teaspoon cream of tartar
2 teaspoons sugar
½ cup shortening, softened
⅔ cup milk

Sift together dry ingredients. Cut in shortening. Add milk; mix until dough just sticks together. Roll out ½ inch thick, cut with biscuit cutter, and place on greased baking sheet. Bake at 400° for 10 to 12 minutes or until light brown.

Chili Con Carne

Makes 6 servings.

- ½ cup chopped onion
- ½ cup chopped green pepper
- ¼ cup chopped celery
- 1 clove garlic, minced
- 1 pound ground beef
- 2½ cups canned tomatoes
- 2 teaspoons sugar
- 2 teaspoons salt
- 1 tablespoon chili powder
- 2½ cups red kidney beans
- 15 sticks vermicelli, broken in small pieces

Sauté onion, green pepper, celery, and garlic until lightly browned. Add meat and sauté until brown, not dark. Add tomatoes, sugar, salt, and chili powder. Cover and bring to a boil. Simmer for 30 minutes. Add kidney beans and vermicelli. Cook for 15 minutes.

Twice-Baked Potatoes

- 4 baking potatoes
- 2 tablespoons hot cream
- 1 egg, well beaten
  Butter to taste
  Salt to taste

Bake potatoes at 425° for 45 minutes. Remove from oven. Cut lengthwise, scoop out centers and mash with remaining ingredients. Beat well. Spoon back into the potato shells. Brush with melted butter. Return to oven and bake 5 to 10 minutes.

Favorite Hamburgers

- 1 pound lean ground beef
- 1 egg
- 1 cup catsup or chili sauce
- 2 teaspoons prepared mustard
- ½ cup chopped onion
- 1 teaspoon salt
  Pepper to taste

Combine ingredients and spread on bun halves. Bake at 375° for 20 minutes.

Oven-Baked Rice

Makes 8 servings.

- 1½ cups uncooked rice
- 3 teaspoons chicken broth
- 3 tablespoons vegetable oil
- 3½ cups boiling water

Combine rice, chicken broth, and vegetable oil in a 2-quart casserole. Pour boiling water over rice and stir with a fork. Cover. Bake at 350° for 40 minutes. To serve, fluff rice with fork.

Macaroni and Cheese

Makes 2 servings.

- 2 cups cooked macaroni
- 5 ounces sharp cheese
- 2 teaspoons butter or margarine
- 1 cup milk

Place macaroni in a buttered casserole. Break cheese into small pieces. Add cheese, butter, and milk to macaroni; mix well. Bake at 375° until cheese has melted.

All-In-One Dinner

Makes 6 servings.

- 1½ pounds ground beef
- 1 cup sliced raw onion
- ¼ cup chopped green pepper
- 2 cups sliced raw potatoes
- 1 cup chopped celery
  Salt and pepper to taste
- 2 cups canned tomatoes
- 4 slices American cheese
  Butter

Sauté ground beef until brown; drain. Place alternate layers of ground beef and fresh vegetables in a greased casserole dish in order listed. Add salt and pepper to each layer. Pour canned tomatoes over all. Top with cheese slices and dot with butter. Cover casserole. Bake at 350° for 1½ hours or until vegetables are done.

Cucumbers in Sour Cream

2 cucumbers, sliced thin
Sour cream

Soak cucumbers in salted water 20 to 30 minutes. Squeeze carefully to remove excess water. Do not mash. Put into a bowl, sprinkle with salt and pepper. Mix with enough sour cream to cover cucumbers.

Vegetable Soup

Makes 8 servings.

1½ pounds beef shank, plus soupbones
8 cups water
2½ tablespoons salt
¼ teaspoon pepper
2 tablespoons minced parsley
½ cup barley
1½ cups cubed carrots
¼ cup chopped onion
½ cup chopped celery
2 cups cooked tomatoes
1½ cups frozen peas

Cut meat into cubes and brown. Place meat, bones, water, seasonings, and parsley in Dutch oven. Cover and cook slowly for 1 hour. Add barley; cook 1 hour. Cool and skim off excess fat. Remove soupbones. Add carrots, onion, celery, and tomatoes. Cook 45 minutes. Add peas and continue cooking 15 minutes.

Butter Cake

Makes 1 9-inch layer cake.

2 cups sugar
¾ cup butter and shortening (half of each)
1 cup milk
4 eggs
2½ cups flour
2 teaspoons baking powder
Pinch salt
1 teaspoon vanilla extract

Put all ingredients into a mixing bowl. Mix 10 minutes at medium speed of electric mixer. Pour batter into 2 greased 9-inch pans and bake at 375° for approximately 40 minutes.

Fantastic Fruit Fluff

Makes 6 to 8 servings.

2 cups milk
1 8-ounce package cream cheese
1 package instant vanilla pudding
1 16-ounce can fruit cocktail, drained
1 cup miniature marshmallows

Gradually add ½ cup of the milk to the cream cheese. Blend in pudding and remaining milk. Beat slowly 1 minute. Stir in fruit and marshmallows. Chill.

Luscious Lemon Pie

1 cup sugar
1¼ cups water
1 tablespoon butter or margarine
¼ cup cornstarch
3 tablespoons cold water
6 tablespoons lemon juice
1 teaspoon grated lemon peel
3 egg yolks
2 tablespoons milk
1 egg white, stiffly beaten
1 baked pie shell

Combine sugar, water and butter. Cook until sugar dissolves. Add cornstarch that has been blended with the cold water. Cook slowly until clear, about 8 minutes. Add lemon juice and grated lemon peel. Cook 2 minutes. Slowly add the egg yolks beaten with the 2 tablespoons of milk. Bring to a boil. Cool. Fold the egg white into the filling. Pour mixture into pie shell. Top with Meringue.

Meringue

½ cup sugar
⅛ teaspoon salt
¼ cup water
⅛ teaspoon cream of tartar
2 egg whites, stiffly beaten
¼ teaspoon almond extract

Cook first 4 ingredients to thread stage (232°). Gradually pour this over egg whites, beating constantly. Continue beating until mixture holds shape. Add almond extract.

Party and Cooking Aids

You'll do the best entertaining and make your guests happiest when you do what you really like to do. So, first of all, decide what kind of party it will be. Formal or informal? Indoors or out? Large or small? What to serve: full-meal, light refreshments, late-evening buffet?

Follow a written plan. You'll save time if you take time to write everything down—from the guest list to the timetable for cooking.

Make a shopping list. Include everything you will need, from cocktail napkins to candles.

Pick a theme. Set the mood. Make your party a little different from anyone else's, whether it's celebrating a birthday, anniversary, job promotion, or just for the fun of it.

Choose guests carefully. They should share some mutual interests. Mix up talkers and listeners. Let the spirit of friendship prevail.

Get out invitations a week or two ahead. Telephone or write a note. In both cases be specific about time, date, place, anything out of the ordinary about dress (sport clothes, costume, black tie), and any special information about the occasion (if it's gift-giving, be explicit).

Plan what you'll serve. Your menu is all-important. No monochromatic menus, please! Get good color contrasts, but make sure foods in the same course do not clash. Contrast hot dishes with cold; soft foods with crisp; bland with strong-flavored. Vary the cooking method, for instance, no completely fried dinners. Enhance a colorless dish with a sauce or colorful garnish.

Choose food that suits the occasion. Be realistic about what you can prepare well. Use recipes that you have already tested. Plan foods that don't require a lot of last-minute fuss. Ideally, choose recipes that can be fully or partially prepared early in the day.

Plan variety. A creamy-sauced food needs something crisp and crunchy. You might add the crunch right in the sauce (with water chestnuts, slivered nuts, or celery); in the vegetable course, or, in a relish tray. Keep a texture contrast throughout the meal, as well as within each course. Top off a heavy meal with a light dessert, and vice versa.

Include both tart and sweet. Save the very sweetest foods for the end of the meal. One strong flavor or spiced dish is usually enough in one meal. Do not repeat flavors in the same meal (such as tomatoes, onions, or nutmeats).

Try new recipes using ingredients you know everyone likes. Even if you can get by serving the same old standbys—don't. Hamburger can be served as Swedish meatballs, individual meat loaves, spaghetti or lasagna. Combining foods is an easy way to create new dishes: mix two different cans of soup together; combine carrots with scallions, peas with dill, green beans with almonds.

Set a schedule for yourself. Plan to be ready one half hour ahead. This will give you time to catch your breath before the guests arrive.

Plan the table setting early. This is fun to do when you have enough time—and aren't polishing silver when you should be putting the finishing touches on the flowers for the centerpiece. Work out a theme or color scheme, and make sure you have all the dishes, linens, and silver to carry it out. Try to set the table in the morning or the night before.

Clear a counter for soiled dishes. Out of sight of guests, please.

COOKERY TERMS

Appetizer: Food served before the first course of a meal.

Brown: To make food a brown color by frying, sautéing, broiling or baking.

Cream: To blend butter and sugar by stirring or beating.

Dice: To cut into small pieces.

Garnish: To add decorative color to food.

Grease: To rub a baking pan with fat, butter or oil.

Knead: To work dough until smooth and pliable.

Marinate: To soak food in a seasoned liquid to flavor and tenderize.

Melt: To liquefy by heat.

Mince: To chop into fine pieces.

Sauté: To cook food quickly with fat, butter or margarine.

Scald: To bring liquid to a temperature just below the boiling point.

Whip: To beat rapidly.

EQUIVALENT AMOUNTS

Apples: 1 pound = 3 medium

Baking chocolate: 1 square = 1 ounce or 5 tablespoons grated

Bread: 1 pound loaf = 18 slices

Butter or margarine: 1 pound = 2 cups; 1 stick or ¼ pound = ½ cup

Cheese (American, Cheddar): 1 pound = 4 cups grated

Cottage cheese: 1 pound = 2 cups

Eggs: 5 whole = 1 cup; 8 whites = about 1 cup; 16 yolks = about 1 cup

Flour, all purpose: 1 pound = 4 cups

Flour, cake: 1 pound = 4¾ cups

Lemon juice: 1 medium lemon = 3 tablespoons juice

Lemon rind: 1 medium lemon = 1 tablespoon grated rind

Noodles: 1 cup raw = 1¼ cups cooked

Macaroni: 1 pound = 3 cups uncooked; 1 cup = 2 cups cooked

Meat: 1 pound = 2 cups diced

Milk, evaporated: 1 6-ounce can = ⅔ cup; 1 14½-ounce can = 1⅔ cups

Potatoes: 1 pound = 3 medium

Rice: 1 pound = 2⅓ cups uncooked; 1 cup raw = 3 cups cooked

Sugar:
Brown—1 pound = 2¼ cups firmly packed;
Confectioners'—1 pound = 3½ cups;
Granulated—1 pound = 2 cups

Tomatoes: 1 pound = 3 medium

Vegetable shortening: 1 pound = 2 cups

CONTENTS OF CANS

Size No.	Cup Amount
300	1¾
1 tall	2
303	2
2	2½
2½	3½
3	4
10	12-13

MEASUREMENTS

1 tablespoon = 3 teaspoons
1 fluid ounce = 2 tablespoons
¼ cup = 4 tablespoons
⅓ cup = 5⅓ tablespoons
½ cup = 8 tablespoons
⅔ cup = 10⅔ tablespoons
¾ cup = 12 tablespoons
1 cup = 16 tablespoons or 8 fluid ounces
1 pint = 2 cups
1 quart = 2 pints or 4 cups
1 pound = 16 ounces
¾ pound = 12 ounces
½ pound = 8 ounces
¼ pound = 4 ounces

Fourth of July

Deviled Eggs

6 hard-cooked eggs
¼ cup mayonnaise
1 teaspoon prepared mustard
½ teaspoon vinegar
¼ teaspoon salt
  White pepper to taste
  Paprika

Cut eggs in half lengthwise. Remove yolks. Mash yolks with remaining ingredients except paprika until mixture is smooth. Fill egg whites with mixture. Sprinkle with paprika.

Marinated Chicken

1 envelope Italian dressing
¼ cup lemon juice
½ cup salad oil
2 frying chickens, cut up
¼ cup instant onion flakes moistened
  with mayonnaise
  Salt, pepper and paprika to taste

Combine first 3 ingredients; pour over chicken and marinate for 4 to 5 hours. Line a baking sheet with foil; grease lightly. Brush meat with a generous coating of mayonnaise-onion mixture. Arrange meat on foil; meat should not touch. Sprinkle with salt, pepper, and paprika. Bake at 350° for 1 hour or until golden brown.

German-Style Potato Salad

Makes 12 servings.

5 pounds salad potatoes
6 slices bacon, diced
¼ cup flour
4 cups water
6 tablespoons sugar
1 teaspoon salt
⅛ teaspoon pepper
1 teaspoon celery salt
¾ cup vinegar
½ cup chopped onion
6 hard-cooked eggs, sliced

Boil potatoes in their skins in salted water until tender. Peel while still warm. Cool. Slice into a large bowl. Fry bacon until crisp. Remove from pan; set aside. Stir flour into bacon fat and blend with a wooden spoon. Add water gradually, stirring until smooth and thick. Add sugar, salt, pepper, and celery salt; simmer and stir until dissolved. Add vinegar and bring to a boil; pour over the sliced potatoes. Add bacon pieces, onion, and sliced eggs; fold until well blended. When cool, cover and refrigerate.

Firecracker Punch

Makes 30 servings.

4 cups cranberry juice
1½ cups sugar
4 cups pineapple juice
1 tablespoon almond extract
2 quarts ginger ale

Combine first 4 ingredients in a punch bowl. Stir until sugar is dissolved. Chill. Add ginger ale just before serving.

Lemon Picnic Cake

1 package yellow cake mix
¾ cup vegetable oil
¾ cup water
1 package instant lemon pudding
4 eggs

Combine all ingredients except eggs and beat 2 minutes. Add eggs, one at a time; beat thoroughly. Pour into greased and floured 9 x 13-inch pan. Bake at 350° for 40 minutes. While hot, prick entire top with a fork. Pour Glaze over cake.

Glaze

2 cups confectioners' sugar
⅓ cup orange juice
2 tablespoons butter, melted
2 tablespoons water

Combine all ingredients until smooth.

Summer Salads

Tomato and Cucumber Salad

Makes 6 servings.

 5 medium tomatoes, sliced
 1 cucumber, thinly sliced
 1 green onion, thinly sliced
 3 tablespoons olive oil
 2 to 3 tablespoons red wine vinegar
 ½ teaspoon salt
 ½ teaspoon crushed oregano
 ¼ teaspoon crushed basil
   Freshly ground pepper
 1 tablespoon minced parsley

Place tomato, cucumber, and green onion in a mixing bowl. Combine remaining ingredients and pour over salad. Chill 1 hour before serving.

Lime Cottage Cheese Dressing

Makes 1 cup.

 ½ cup mayonnaise
 ½ cup small curd cottage cheese
 2 tablespoons milk
 1 tablespoon sugar
 ½ teaspoon grated lime rind
 1 tablespoon lime juice

Combine all ingredients in a blender until smooth. Chill. Serve on a citrus fruit salad.

Smorgasbord Slaw

Makes 3 quarts.

 2 cups sugar
 1 cup vinegar
 ½ cup water
 1 tablespoon salt
 1 large cabbage, sliced thin
 2 medium red peppers, chopped
 2 medium green peppers, chopped
 ½ bunch celery, chopped
 1½ teaspoons mustard seed
 1½ teaspoons celery seed

Combine sugar, vinegar, and water in a saucepan; boil 5 minutes. Cool. Sprinkle salt over cabbage. Allow to stand 1 hour. Add peppers, celery, mustard seed, celery seed, and cooled vinegar mixture. Mix well. Chill.

Hot Chicken Salad

 1 cup chopped celery
 2 cups cubed, cooked chicken breast
 1 cup cooked rice
 1 10¾-ounce can cream of chicken soup, undiluted
 1 teaspoon fresh minced onion
 1 teaspoon lemon juice
 1 teaspoon salt
 ¾ cup mayonnaise
 ½ cup sliced water chestnuts
 1 cup crushed cornflakes
 ½ cup sliced almonds

Sauté celery for a few minutes. Mix all ingredients except cornflakes and almonds and place in a casserole. Sprinkle cornflakes and almonds over the top. Bake at 350° for 25 to 30 minutes.

Note: Make ahead and refrigerate until ready to use. Do not add the cornflakes and almonds until dish is ready for the oven. If salad is cold increase cooking time 20 to 30 minutes.

Pineapple-Mint Salad

 1 3-ounce package lime-flavored gelatin
 ¼ cup sour cream
 2 tablespoons sugar
 2 teaspoons mint flavoring
 2½ cups canned pineapple chunks, drained

Prepare gelatin according to package directions. Add sour cream, sugar, and mint. Allow to thicken slightly and stir in pineapple.

Pineapple-Marshmallow Salad

 3 eggs
 ⅓ cup flour
 ½ cup pineapple juice
 ½ cup sugar
 ½ pint whipping cream, whipped
 2 cups small marshmallows
 2½ cups canned chunk pineapple, drained
   Maraschino cherries

Combine eggs, flour, pineapple juice and sugar in top of a double boiler. Cook until thick. Cool. Add whipped cream. Fold in marshmallows, pineapple and cherries. Chill.

Marshmallow Waldorf Salad

Makes 4 to 6 servings.

   3 cups cubed apples
   1 tablespoon lemon juice
   1 cup miniature marshmallows
   1 cup chopped celery
  ¼ cup chopped walnuts
     Mayonnaise
     Lettuce

Sprinkle apples with lemon juice. Add marshmallows, celery, nuts and enough mayonnaise to moisten. Toss lightly. Serve on lettuce.

Zesty Coleslaw

Makes 6 to 8 servings.

   4 teaspoons vinegar
   2 teaspoons sugar
   1 teaspoon celery salt
   1 teaspoon dillweed
   4 cups shredded cabbage
   1 green pepper, minced, optional
   2 pimiento strips, minced, optional
  ½ cup mayonnaise or salad dressing

Mix all ingredients well; add more mayonnaise if necessary. Chill.

Mixed Vegetable Salad

   2 1¼-pound packages frozen mixed vegetables
   1 cup diced celery
   1 medium onion, diced
   1 medium green pepper, diced

Cook frozen vegetables until tender. Drain. Add remaining ingredients. Pour Dressing over vegetables and mix well.

Dressing

1½ cups sugar
  ¾ cup white vinegar
  ¾ cup salad oil
   1 teaspoon paprika
   2 tablespoons water
     Salt to taste

Combine all ingredients in a saucepan; bring to a boil. Cool.

Lime Cucumber Salad

Makes 6 servings.

   1 package lime-flavored gelatin
   1 cup boiling water
  ¼ cup vinegar
   1 teaspoon salt
   1 teaspoon grated onion
   1 cup sour cream
   1 medium cucumber, coarsely grated
     Lettuce

Dissolve gelatin in the boiling water. Add vinegar, salt and onion. Chill until gelatin begins to thicken. Stir in sour cream and cucumber. Pour into 6 individual molds (or loaf pan about 12 x 5 x 3 inches). Chill until firm. Unmold onto lettuce bed.

Shrimp Potato Salad

  ½ pound canned shrimp, drained
   2 cups diced, cold cooked potatoes
  ⅔ cup chopped celery
  ¼ cup diced pickles
   3 hard-cooked eggs, diced
  ¼ cup shredded cheese
   2 tablespoons chopped onion
  ½ cup salad dressing
   1 teaspoon salt
     Dash pepper

Combine all ingredients; chill.

Creamed Ham Supreme

   4 tablespoons butter
   2 cups milk
  ¼ cup flour
   1 cup diced ham
   1 cup diced cheese
     Salt
     Paprika

Melt butter in a saucepan; blend in milk and flour and stir until smooth. Stir until mixture begins to thicken. Stir in ham, cheese, and salt to taste. Dust with paprika. Serve over poached eggs on toast or use over broccoli, asparagus or Brussels sprouts.

Weekend Cookout

Oregano Dip

1 teaspoon crushed oregano
½ teaspoon grated onion
¼ teaspoon salt
　Few drops Tabasco sauce
1 cup sour cream

Blend all ingredients into sour cream. Cover and chill.

Spiced Ice Tea

Makes 12 servings.

1 cup sugar
1 cup water
1 whole nutmeg
2 sticks cinnamon
1 orange, studded with whole cloves
2 cups orange juice
¼ cup lemon juice
3 cups double-strength iced tea

Combine sugar, water, nutmeg, and cinnamon in a saucepan. Simmer 10 minutes. Add the orange. Cover; cool and strain. Add orange juice, lemon juice, and iced tea. Serve over ice cubes in tall glasses.

Garden Potato Salad

Makes 8 to 10 servings.

2½ pounds small potatoes, cooked, peeled and sliced
1 medium onion, chopped
1 cucumber, peeled, chopped, seeds removed
1 cup chopped celery
1 cup chopped fresh tomatoes
½ cup sliced radishes
5 hard-cooked eggs
1 teaspoon salt
½ teaspoon pepper
　Garlic, celery salt and onion salt to taste
1½ cups mayonnaise or salad dressing
½ cup milk
　Paprika

In a large bowl combine potatoes, the vegetables, 3 chopped, hard-cooked eggs, and seasonings. Combine mayonnaise with milk. Pour over vegetables; mix well. Garnish with the 2 remaining eggs, sliced, and paprika.

Charcoal-Broiled Sirloin Steak

1 sirloin steak
⅓ cup salad oil
⅓ cup red wine vinegar
2 cloves garlic, crushed
1 teaspoon basil
½ teaspoon salt
½ teaspoon pepper

Trim excess fat from steak. Slash fat edge of steak at 1-inch intervals. Place steak in a pan large enough to allow steak to remain flat. Combine remaining ingredients. Mix and pour over steak. Cover. Chill 2 to 3 hours, turning several times. Start charcoal fire 30 to 40 minutes ahead of time, until coals are glowing and covered with gray ash. Rub hot grill with a bit of the fat trimmed from steak. Broil a 1½- to 2-inch steak 5 to 6 inches above coals. Place a 1-inch steak on a rack 4½ to 5 inches above coals. Broil first side, turn and brush with marinade, if desired. Broil second side until done.

Note: To test steak for degree of doneness, cut a small slash with a sharp knife in center of steak.

Fudge Treats

1 cup flour
1 cup sugar
½ teaspoon baking soda
½ teaspoon salt
½ teaspoon vanilla extract
¼ cup shortening, softened
2 eggs
2 squares baking chocolate
⅓ cup water
½ cup dairy sour cream
1 cup (6-ounces) semisweet chocolate chips
½ cup chopped nuts

Combine all ingredients, except chocolate chips and nuts, in a mixing bowl. Beat at medium speed 2 minutes. Spread in a greased pan. Sprinkle chocolate chips and nuts on top. Bake at 350° for 25 to 30 minutes or until top springs back when touched in center. Cool. Sprinkle on confectioners' sugar.

SPICED ICED TEA

- 2 quarts water
- 12 single tea bags
- 1 c. water
- 1½ c. sugar
- ½ c. strained orange juice
- 1 c. strained lemon juice
- 12 cloves
- 2 sticks cinnamon

Boil 2 quarts water. Add tea bags and steep 5 minutes. Remove tea bags. In a small pot bring 1 cup water and sugar to a boil. Remove from heat and add juices and spices. Add spiced mixture to steeped tea. Serve over ice in tall glasses.

Accompaniments

Corn Relish

Makes 6 pints.

12 large ears corn, uncooked
 1 large cabbage, chopped
 3 large onions, chopped
 2 green peppers, chopped
 1 red pepper, chopped
1½ to 2 tablespoons salt
 3 pints vinegar
 2 cups sugar
 1 tablespoon celery seed
 1 tablespoon dry mustard
 1 teaspoon turmeric
 ¼ cup flour

Cut corn from cobs. Mix vegetables and salt. Add half of the vinegar; bring to a boil. Combine sugar, seasonings, and flour. Add remaining vinegar; stir until smooth. Cook until thickened. Add to vegetables and cook for 30 minutes or until vegetables are tender. Pour into hot sterilized jars and seal.

Sweet Relish

Makes 5 to 6 pints.

 6 pounds (22 medium) green tomatoes, quartered, stem ends removed
 3 onions, quartered
 2 green peppers, quartered
1⅔ cups granulated sugar
1¾ cups white vinegar
 ½ teaspoon ground cinnamon
 ½ teaspoon ground allspice
 ½ teaspoon turmeric
 ¼ teaspoon cayenne pepper
1½ teaspoons celery seed
 3 tablespoons salt

Put all vegetables through medium blade of food grinder. Drain excess liquid. Bring sugar, vinegar, and seasonings to a boil in a large kettle. Add vegetables. Simmer 10 minutes, stirring occasionally. Continue to simmer relish while quickly packing one hot sterilized jar at a time. Fill to within ½ inch from the top. Vinegar solution should be covering vegetables. Seal each jar immediately.

Tomato Relish

 5 medium tomatoes, peeled, seeded and diced
 1 medium green pepper, diced
 1 medium onion, diced
 1 rib celery, diced
 1 small cucumber, diced
 1 tablespoon horseradish
 1 teaspoon salt
 ½ cup wine vinegar
 ¼ cup sugar
 1 teaspoon mustard seed
 ⅛ teaspoon ground cloves
   Dash black pepper

Combine vegetables, horseradish, and salt. Cover; let stand at room temperature for 2 hours. Drain well. Pour vinegar, sugar, mustard seed, cloves, and pepper over vegetables, mixing well. Chill for 6 hours or overnight. Keeps 4 to 6 days.

Red Pepper Relish

 1 peck red peppers, trimmed and seeds removed
 2 ounces mustard seed
 3 pounds sugar
 3 pints white vinegar

Grind peppers with a fine cutter. Rinse mustard seed and soak in hot water 2 to 3 hours; drain. Combine all ingredients. Cook over low heat until mixture jells; stirring often to prevent scorching.

Three-Bean Salad

 1 can green beans
 1 can yellow beans
 1 can kidney beans
 1 medium onion, minced
   Salt and pepper to taste
 ¾ cup salad oil
 ½ cup wine vinegar
 2 hard-cooked eggs, minced

Mix together all ingredients. Place in a covered bowl and marinate overnight in refrigerator. Salad will keep for a week, if refrigerated.

Bread-and-Butter Pickles

Makes 7 pints.

25 medium cucumbers, sliced
12 onions, sliced
½ cup salt
2 cups sugar
2 teaspoons turmeric
1 quart vinegar
2 teaspoons mustard seed
2 teaspoons celery seed

Soak cucumbers and onions in salted ice water for 3 hours. Combine remaining ingredients; heat to boiling. Drain cucumbers and onions and add to vinegar mixture. Heat for 2 minutes; do not boil. Fill clean jars; seal.

Pickled Beets

48 small red beets
2 cups cider vinegar
4 cups water
3 cups sugar
1 lemon, thinly sliced, optional
2 sticks cinnamon
1 teaspoon whole cloves
1 teaspoon whole allspice, optional

Cook beets; drain and peel. Make a syrup of vinegar, water, sugar, lemon, and spices. Simmer 15 minutes. Place beets in sterilized jars. Pour hot syrup over beets to within ½ inch of top of jar. Seal.

Icicle Pickles

Makes 6 pints.

3 pounds 4-inch cucumbers, cleaned and cut in spears
6 small onions, quartered
6 5-inch pieces celery
1 tablespoon mustard seed
1 quart vinegar
¼ cup salt
2½ cups sugar
1 cup water

Soak cucumber spears in ice water 3 to 5 hours. Drain and pack into pint jars. To each jar add 1 quartered onion, 1 piece of celery, ⅓ teaspoon mustard seed. Combine vinegar, salt, sugar, and water in a saucepan; bring to a boil. Pour solution over cucumbers to within ½ inch of top of jars. Seal.

Refrigerator Pickles

12 to 15 6-inch cucumbers, sliced
3 onions, sliced

Wash and sterilize 3 large quart jars. Layer cucumbers and onions in the jars; pack well. Pour Syrup over cucumbers and onions; screw on lids. Refrigerate at least 5 days before using. Store pickles in refrigerator.

Syrup

4 cups sugar
4 cups vinegar
½ cup pickling salt
1⅓ teaspoons celery seed
1⅓ teaspoons turmeric
1⅓ teaspoons mustard seed

Mix sugar, vinegar, and spices together. Do not heat. Stir well.

Jerusalem Artichoke Pickles

1 gallon Jerusalem artichokes, washed, scraped and left whole
3 quarts vinegar
3 pounds sugar
2 tablespoons turmeric
1 tablespoon ground ginger
1 tablespoon mustard seed
1 tablespoon celery seed
2 to 3 sticks cinnamon

Pack artichokes into sterilized jars as tightly as possible. In a saucepan, combine remaining ingredients. Cook for ½ hour over low heat. Cool syrup until slightly warm. Pour over artichokes and seal jars.

Note: Be sure the syrup is only warm, as it will shrivel the artichokes if too hot.

Lime Party Salad

Makes 12 servings.

- 16 marshmallows
- 1 cup milk
- 1 package lime-flavored gelatin
- 2 3-ounce packages cream cheese, softened
- 2½ cups canned crushed pineapple and juice
- 1 cup whipping cream, whipped
- ⅔ cup mayonnaise

Melt marshmallows and milk in the top of a double boiler. Pour over the gelatin; stirring until the gelatin dissolves. Add the cream cheese and stir until the cheese melts. Fold in pineapple. Cool. Blend together whipped cream and mayonnaise; fold into mixture. Chill until firm.

Moist Chocolate Cake

Makes 2 9-inch cakes.

- 2 teaspoons baking soda
- ½ cup sour milk
- 2 cups sugar
- ½ cup vegetable shortening
- 2 eggs
- ¼ teaspoon salt
- 2 cups flour
- 1 teaspoon vanilla extract
- 4 tablespoons cocoa
- 1 cup boiling water

Dissolve baking soda in the sour milk. Mix all ingredients except boiling water in a mixing bowl. Add boiling water; mix. Grease 2 9-inch pans; dust with flour. Bake at 375° for 30 to 35 minutes.

Super Butterwhip Frosting

- ½ cup vegetable shortening
- ½ cup butter or margarine
- 1 cup granulated sugar
- ¾ cup milk
- Dash salt
- 1 teaspoon vanilla extract

Cream shortening, butter, and sugar in a small bowl of an electric mixer; set aside. In a small saucepan heat the milk until very hot; do not let it boil. Add the milk to the creamed mixture slowly, 1 tablespoon at a time, beating well after each addition. Add the salt and vanilla. Continue beating until mixture is soft like whipped cream.

Slush

Makes 25 to 30 servings.

- ½ gallon fruit sherbet
- 2 quarts ginger ale or white soda
- ⅓ 46-ounce can unsweetened pineapple juice

Combine all ingredients.

Tasty Party Buns

Makes 12 servings.

- 1 pound bologna
- ¾ pound American cheese
- ¼ cup prepared mustard
- ⅓ cup salad dressing
- 1 tablespoon minced onion
- 2 tablespoons chopped sweet pickle
- 12 hot dog buns
- Butter

Grind meat and cheese into a mixing bowl. Add mustard, salad dressing, onion, and chopped pickle; mix well. Cut buns in half, spread with butter and fill with meat mixture. Wrap each bun in foil. Heat at 325° for 25 minutes.

Burger Pizza

- 1 cup biscuit mix
- Vegetable oil
- 1 pound ground chuck
- Salt and pepper to taste
- Garlic salt to taste
- 1 teaspoon dried oregano
- 1 8-ounce can tomato sauce
- 1 tablespoon parsley
- ¼ pound Swiss cheese, cut into 1-inch strips

Prepare biscuit dough according to package directions. Roll flat onto a pizza pan and brush with vegetable oil. In a skillet brown beef; mix in salt, pepper, garlic salt, oregano, and tomato sauce. Spoon over dough. Sprinkle with parsley. Arrange cheese strips on top like spokes of a wheel. Bake at 400° for 20 minutes or until cheese melts. Cut into wedges. Serve hot.

Teenager's Party

Cheese Dainties

½ pound grated sharp cheese
½ pound margarine
2 cups flour
1 teaspoon salt
Dash red pepper

Mix above ingredients well with hands and shape into balls a little smaller than a walnut. Press lightly onto ungreased baking sheets and bake at 375° for 8 to 10 minutes until light tan.

Barbecue Burgers

Makes 6 to 8 servings.

½ pound ground beef
2 tablespoons chopped onion
2 tablespoons chopped green pepper
1 rib celery, diced
½ cup catsup
½ cup water
1 tablespoon vinegar
1½ teaspoons Worcestershire sauce
½ teaspoon prepared mustard
1 tablespoon brown sugar
½ teaspoon salt
⅛ teaspoon allspice

Lightly brown beef; add onion, green pepper, and celery. Sauté. Combine remaining ingredients and pour over meat. Cover pan tightly; simmer for 30 minutes. Serve hot over toasted buns.

French-Fried Onion Rings

1½ cups flour
1 teaspoon baking powder
1½ teaspoons salt
2 eggs, beaten
1 cup milk
1 teaspoon shortening, melted
Bermuda onions, thinly sliced

Sift dry ingredients together. Stir eggs, milk, and shortening into flour mixture; beat until smooth. Separate onions into rings; dip into batter. Deep fry in hot oil about 2 minutes or until golden brown. Do not crowd.

Tossed Fruit Salad

2 cups shredded cabbage
1 cup diced oranges
1 cup sliced, unpeeled Delicious apples
2 teaspoons grated onion
1 tablespoon lemon juice
½ teaspoon sugar
⅓ cup mayonnaise

Combine all ingredients and toss lightly. Serve on crisp salad greens.

Party Dip

Makes 2½ cups.

1 envelope onion soup mix
1 pint sour cream
1 medium tomato, chopped
1 small green pepper, diced
¼ teaspoon dillweed

Blend soup with sour cream. Add remaining ingredients. Chill at least 1 hour. Serve with assorted chips and breadsticks.

Banana Split Dessert

Makes 25 servings.

Graham cracker crumbs
3 or 4 bananas, sliced
½ gallon Neapolitan ice cream
1 cup chopped walnuts
½ cup butter
1 cup chocolate chips
2 cups confectioners' sugar
1½ cups evaporated milk
1 pint whipping cream, whipped
¼ cup confectioners' sugar
1 teaspoon vanilla extract

Cover an 11 x 15-inch pan with graham cracker crumbs. Arrange bananas over crumbs. Slice ice cream ½ inch thick and place over bananas. Sprinkle with nuts. Place in freezer until firm. Melt butter and chocolate chips over low heat. Add sugar and milk; cook until thick, stirring constantly. Cool and pour over crumb mixture. Chill. Whip cream. Add the ¼ cup confectioners' sugar and vanilla; pour over all. Freeze. Serve in slices or squares.

Fondue Fun

A fondue party can create much fun. It is perfect for teens, small informal dinner parties, and cookouts. All you need is the ingredients and the guests. Allow the guests the fun of preparing their own meal at the table; each diner becomes his own chef. Be sure to warn guests that the fondue forks become very hot and advise them to transfer the cooked food to a dinner fork, dipping into sauces.

In planning a fondue party, give free rein to your imagination. Serve a tossed green salad, crunchy dinner rolls, and a simple dessert of fresh fruit and cheese.

Food to Fondue

Serve with assorted sauces.

Beef tenderloin cubes
Fresh whole mushrooms
Cooked shrimp
Cherry tomatoes
Green pepper wedges
Ham pieces
Small whole onions
Potato cubes
Pineapple chunks
Broccoli

Cheese Fondue

Makes 4 cups.

1¼ cups dry white wine
1 clove garlic, chopped
8 ounces natural Swiss cheese, cut into pieces
¼ cup flour
2 10¾-ounce cans condensed Cheddar cheese soup
French bread or whole wheat bread, cubed

Heat wine and garlic in a saucepan or fondue pot to simmering. Combine cheese and flour. Gradually blend into wine. Heat until cheese is melted, stirring occasionally. Blend in soup. Heat, stirring until smooth. Dip bread into fondue.

Chocolate Fondue

6 3-ounce bars of sweet baker's chocolate
¼ cup plus 2 tablespoons cream
¼ cup kirsch or brandy
1 tablespoon instant (not freeze-dried) coffee
⅛ teaspoon ground cinnamon

In a fondue pot or heavy saucepan over low heat, melt the chocolate in the cream. Add remaining ingredients and stir. To serve, provide small plates, long-handled forks and generous helpings of whole strawberries, pecan halves, banana slices, orange sections or a pound cake cut into cubes.

Beef Fondue

Cooking oil
1 teaspoon salt
2 pounds beef tenderloin, cut into 1-inch cubes

Place metal fondue pot in center of table. Heat oil to 425° or until a cube of bread browns quickly. Add salt. Pour into fondue pot over fondue burner. Use long-handled, two-prong fondue forks to spear meat cubes. Fry the cubes in the hot oil to desired doneness. Remove to a plate and dip in sauce with a dinner fork.

Dipping Sauce

1 beef bouillon cube
⅔ cup boiling water
2 tablespoons flour
2 tablespoons butter, melted
½ cup dairy sour cream
1 3-ounce can mushrooms, drained and minced
2 teaspoons Worcestershire sauce
Salt and pepper to taste

Dissolve bouillon in the water. Stir flour into the butter. Add bouillon and stir while cooking until thick and bubbly. Add sour cream, mushrooms, and Worcestershire sauce. Season to taste. Serve while hot.

Dainty Rolls

Makes 50 small rolls.

- 2 **cups warm water (110 to 115°)**
- 1 **package dry yeast**
- 1 **teaspoon salt**
- ¾ **cup sugar**
- 1 **egg**
- 6 **cups flour**
- ¼ **cup vegetable oil**
- **Butter**

Combine warm water and yeast in a large bowl; let stand about 5 minutes. Add salt, sugar, and egg to the yeast mixture; mix. Sift in 3 cups of the flour, mixing well. Add oil. Mix in about 3 more cups flour. Oil top and let rise in a warm place until double in size. Knead until satiny; roll out ¼ inch thick, oil top and cut out as for biscuits. Place a pat of butter on top of each dough round; fold over. Place in a shallow, well-oiled pan. Let rise until double. Bake at 450° for 12 minutes.

Note: To freeze, reduce baking time to 8 minutes. When ready to serve, place rolls in oven and brown.

Beef Stroganoff

Makes 6 servings.

- ½ **pound fresh mushrooms, sliced**
- 1 **large onion, chopped**
- ¼ **cup butter**
- 2 **pounds round steak, ¼- to ½-inch thick**
  Flour
- 1 **teaspoon salt**
  Dash pepper
- 1 **10½-ounce can consommé, diluted with water to make 2 cups**
- 1 **cup sour cream**

Sauté mushrooms and onion in 2 tablespoons butter and remove from pan. Remove fat from steak and cut steak into strips. Melt remaining 2 tablespoons butter in skillet; brown meat, adding flour to coat thoroughly. Add salt, pepper, consommé, and water. Combine and bake at 375° for 1½ to 2 hours. Fifteen minutes before serving, remove from oven and stir in sour cream. Heat well. Serve over noodles or rice.

Candy Apples

- 10 **medium apples**
- 10 **wooden skewers**
- 2½ **cups sugar**
- ½ **cup water**
- 1 **teaspoon vanilla extract**
- ½ **cup light corn syrup**
- 1 **teaspoon red food coloring**

Wash and dry apples; insert skewers in the stem end. Combine sugar, water, vanilla, corn syrup, and food coloring and cook in a large, deep pan. During cooking the crystals which form on the pan should not be stirred into the candy. Continue cooking without stirring to hard crack stage (280°). Remove from heat, hold apples by skewers and dip into syrup. Place on buttered platter to cool.

Halloween Date Cake

- ½ **cup shortening**
- 1 **cup sugar**
- ½ **teaspoon salt**
- 1 **teaspoon ground cinnamon**
- ½ **teaspoon ground cloves**
- 1 **cup warm water**
- 1½ **cups flour, sifted**
- 1 **teaspoon baking soda**
- 1 **cup chopped dates**
- ½ **cup chopped walnuts**

Combine first 6 ingredients in a saucepan; mix well. Slowly bring to a boil and boil for 30 seconds. Cool. Sift together flour and baking soda. Add to cooled liquid, beating well. Fold in dates and nuts. Grease a 15½ x 10½-inch pan; line with waxed paper and grease paper. Distribute batter evenly in pan. Bake at 350° for 30 to 35 minutes or until top springs back when lightly touched. When cool, frost with Orange Butter Frosting.

Orange Butter Frosting

- **Rind of ½ orange, grated**
- **Juice of ½ orange, strained**
- 2 **tablespoons butter, melted**
- 1 **tablespoon heavy cream**
- 4 **cups confectioners' sugar, sifted**

Combine first 4 ingredients. Gradually add sugar. Beat until creamy. Spread on cake.

Harvest Time

Apple Cider Punch

Makes 20 to 25 servings.

- 1 quart apple cider
- 2 cups cranberry juice
- 1 cup orange juice
- 1 12-ounce can apricot nectar
- 1 cup sugar
- 2 sticks cinnamon

Combine all ingredients in a large saucepan; simmer for 20 minutes. Garnish punch with floating orange slices, decorated with cloves.

Chocolate Intrigue

- 3 cups sifted all-purpose flour
- 2 teaspoons baking powder
- ½ teaspoon salt
- 1 cup butter
- 2 cups sugar
- 3 eggs
- 1 cup milk
- 1½ teaspoons vanilla extract
- ¾ cup chocolate syrup
- ¼ teaspoon baking soda
- ¼ teaspoon peppermint extract, optional

Sift together flour, baking powder, and salt. Cream butter, gradually adding sugar. Blend in one egg at a time, beating well after each addition. Combine milk and vanilla. Add alternately with the dry ingredients, beginning and ending with dry ingredients. Blend well after each addition. Pour ⅔ of the batter into a well greased and lightly floured tube pan. Add the syrup, soda, and peppermint to remaining batter; mix well. Spoon chocolate batter over white batter. Do not mix. Bake at 350° for 65 to 70 minutes. When cake is cool, frost with Chocolate Frosting.

Chocolate Frosting

- 4 ounces unsweetened chocolate, melted
- 3 tablespoons butter, softened
- 1 egg, lightly beaten
- 2½ cups sifted confectioners' sugar
- ⅓ cup milk

Combine all ingredients. Beat until of spreading consistency.

Pumpkin Bread

Makes 2 loaves.

- 4 cups flour
- 3 cups sugar
- 1 teaspoon baking powder
- 2 teaspoons baking soda
- 1 teaspoon ground cinnamon
- 1 teaspoon ground nutmeg
- 1 teaspoon ground allspice
- ½ teaspoon ground cloves
- 1 cup vegetable oil
- 1 14½-ounce can pumpkin
- ⅔ cup cold water
- 4 eggs

Sift dry ingredients into a large mixing bowl. Make a well in the flour and pour in vegetable oil. Add pumpkin and cold water; blend well. Add eggs, one at a time, beating well after each addition. Pour batter into 2 well greased and floured loaf pans. Bake at 350° for 1 hour.

Baked Zucchini Slices

- 2 cups sliced zucchini, cooked with 1 garlic clove
- 2 slices bread, cubed
- ½ cup grated yellow cheese
- 1 egg, beaten
- 2 tablespoons chopped parsley
- 2 tablespoons salad oil

Drain cooked squash. Combine all ingredients. Bake at 350° for 30 minutes.

Soft Molasses Cookies

Makes 5 to 6 dozen cookies.

- 1 cup molasses
- 1 cup sugar
- 5 cups flour
- 1 cup vegetable shortening, softened
- 1 egg, lightly beaten

Combine all ingredients and mix well. Roll out on floured board; cut with round cookie cutter. Bake at 400° for 8 to 10 minutes or until done.

Note: If dropped cookies are preferred, use less flour and drop from spoon.

Liver and Vegetable Sauté

½ pound sliced beef liver
2 tablespoons flour
3 tablespoons butter or margarine
1 cup sliced mushrooms
1 small green pepper, sliced
1 8-ounce can stewed tomatoes
¾ teaspoon salt
¼ teaspoon chili powder
Dash cayenne pepper
Lemon juice

Dust liver with flour. Heat liver in butter until brown on both sides, about 5 minutes. Stir in remaining ingredients, except lemon juice; heat to boiling. Reduce heat; simmer until liver is done, about 10 minutes. Sprinkle with lemon juice.

Orange Marmalade

5 oranges, chopped
2 grapefruit, chopped
12 cups cold water
8½ cups sugar
Juice of 2 lemons

Combine oranges, grapefruit, and water in a large kettle; boil for 1 hour, or until fruit is soft. Add sugar and boil for 45 minutes. Add lemon juice; boil until thick. Pour into glasses and seal with paraffin.

Cranberry Squares

1 cup packed brown sugar
½ teaspoon salt
1 cup flour
1 cup quick-cooking rolled oats
¾ cup margarine, melted
1 can whole cranberry sauce

Mix sugar, salt, flour, and oats. Pour margarine over mixture and blend. Spread half of mixture in an 8- or 9-inch square pan. Spread cranberry sauce over bottom layer. Top with remaining half of mixture. Bake at 350° for 45 minutes. Serve with whipped cream or ice cream.

Zucchini Bread

Makes 2 loaves.

3 eggs
1 cup cooking oil
2 cups sugar
3 cups peeled, grated zucchini
2 teaspoons vanilla extract
3 cups flour
¼ teaspoon baking powder
1 teaspoon baking soda
1 teaspoon salt
3 teaspoons ground cinnamon
½ cup chopped nuts

Beat eggs until light and foamy. Add next 4 ingredients; mix lightly. In a separate bowl mix dry ingredients. Add to zucchini mixture and blend. Add nuts. Put in 2 greased and floured loaf pans and bake at 325° for 1 hour. Remove from pans immediately and cool on racks.

Note: This bread may be frozen for later use.

Harvest Casserole

3 pounds lean ground beef
1 large onion, chopped
2 cups chopped celery
1 8-ounce package egg noodles, cooked
1 13-ounce can evaporated milk
3 10¾-ounce cans cream of mushroom soup
¾ pound Velveeta cheese, grated

Sauté ground beef and onion; drain fat. Sauté celery in a small amount of margarine over low heat. Mix all ingredients and spoon into one large casserole or several small ones. Bake at 350° until bubbly.

Note: This casserole makes approximately 1 gallon. It freezes well either before or after baking.

Toasted Pumpkin Seeds

Spread 2 cups pumpkin seeds, washed and drained, on a baking sheet; sprinkle with salt. Toast at 350° for 15 minutes.

Thanksgiving

Corn and Peppers

- 2 tablespoons chopped onion
- 2 tablespoons chopped green pepper
- 2 tablespoons butter or margarine
- 2 tablespoons flour
- 2 cups cooked corn
- 1 cup milk
- ½ teaspoon salt
- ½ cup cracker crumbs
- 2 tablespoons margarine, melted

Sauté onion and green pepper in the butter until soft. Add flour, corn, milk, and salt. Spoon into a baking dish. Stir cracker crumbs with melted butter; spread on top of corn mixture. Bake at 350° for 20 to 30 minutes or until brown.

Sweet Potato Bake

Makes 6 to 8 servings.

- 1 9-ounce can pineapple chunks and juice
- 5 cups mashed sweet potatoes or yams
- ½ teaspoon salt
- 2 tablespoons butter or margarine
- 1 small package miniature marshmallows
- ⅓ cup pecan halves

Cut pineapple chunks in half. Combine pineapple with juice, potatoes, salt, and butter. Place half of mixture in a buttered casserole. Top with half of the marshmallows. Add remaining half of potato mixture. Arrange pecans on top. Cover and bake at 350° for 30 minutes. Remove cover about 10 minutes before serving. Add remaining marshmallows.

Note: This can be made the night before and refrigerated. Add the nuts just before baking.

Turkey Stuffing

Makes enough for a 15- to 18-pound turkey.

- 4 quarts day-old bread cubes
- 3 cups boiled, peeled, and sliced potatoes
- 3 or 4 ribs celery, diced
- ½ cup diced onion
- 1½ teaspoons salt
- ½ teaspoon pepper

Combine all ingredients. Do not use fresh bread. Fill cavity lightly (do not pack) to prevent stuffing from becoming gummy.

Note: Potatoes cooked with skins give better flavor.

Cranberry Crunch

- 1 cup rolled oats
- ¾ cup brown sugar
- ½ cup flour
- ½ cup coconut
- ⅓ cup butter
- 1 16-ounce can whole cranberry sauce
- 1 tablespoon lemon juice

Mix first 5 ingredients together, cutting in butter. Place half of the mixture in a greased 9-inch pan. Add whole cranberry sauce with lemon juice. Top with other half of crunch mixture. Bake at 350° for 45 minutes.

Miniature Pecan Pies

- 1 3-ounce package cream cheese, softened
- ½ cup margarine, softened
- 1 cup flour

Combine cream cheese and margarine; blend well. Add flour and mix thoroughly. Chill overnight. Divide pastry into 24 balls and press into miniature muffin tins, covering bottom and sides. Spoon Pecan Filling into pastry shells. Bake at 325° for 25 minutes. Cool in pans; turn out onto waxed paper.

Pecan Filling

- 1 egg, lightly beaten
- ¾ cup firmly packed light brown sugar
- 1 tablespoon margarine, melted
- 1 teaspoon vanilla extract
  Dash salt
- ⅔ cup coarsely broken pecans

Combine all ingredients; mix well.

Note: For variety use coconut and dates in place of pecans. Pastry shells can be baked and then filled with jellies or marmalade.

Autumn Favorites

Autumn Pumpkin Cake

1 package yellow cake mix
4 eggs, lightly beaten
¾ cup sugar
½ cup salad oil
1 cup cooked or canned pumpkin
¼ cup water
1 teaspoon ground cinnamon
   Dash ground nutmeg

Combine all ingredients in a large mixing bowl. Beat 5 minutes with electric mixer. Pour into a greased and floured tube pan. Bake at 350° for 35 minutes or until done. Frost with Cream Cheese Icing.

Cream Cheese Icing

1 3-ounce package cream cheese, softened
½ cup margarine, melted
1 16-ounce box confectioners' sugar
1 teaspoon vanilla extract

Beat cream cheese and margarine until well blended. Add sugar and vanilla; beat until smooth.

Gingerbread

½ cup butter, softened
½ cup sugar
1 egg, beaten
1 cup molasses
2½ cups sifted flour
1½ teaspoons baking soda
1 teaspoon ground cinnamon
1 teaspoon ground ginger
½ teaspoon ground cloves
½ teaspoon salt
1 cup boiling water
4 ounces miniature marshmallows

Cream butter and sugar. Add egg and molasses; beat until blended. Combine dry ingredients; add to mixture alternately with boiling water, stirring after each addition. Place in 2 greased 8-inch pans and bake at 350° for 45 minutes. Remove from oven. Place 1 layer on oven proof dish. Arrange marshmallows on top. Cover with second layer. Return to oven and bake until marshmallows melt. Serve hot.

Apple Slices

2 cups flour
1 teaspoon salt
⅔ cup butter, softened
1 egg yolk, beaten
½ cup milk
   Sliced apples
   Ground cinnamon
⅔ cup sugar
   Butter
1 egg white, beaten

Combine flour, salt, and butter. Add egg yolk and milk; mix well. Divide dough in half; roll each half thin on a floured surface. Place one half on a buttered baking sheet. Add apples, cinnamon, sugar, and bits of butter. Top with remaining dough. Spread egg white over dough. Sprinkle with sugar. Bake at 350° until brown and apples are tender.

Carrot Marmalade

Scald several carrots and remove skins. Put carrots through a food chopper. To each pint of pulp, add juice and grated rind of 1 lemon and 1¾ cups sugar. Pour into a saucepan. Allow to stand overnight. Boil mixture until clear; spoon into jelly glasses.

Baked Apple Butter

10 pounds apples
1½ quarts cider
1 tablespoon ground cloves
1 tablespoon ground cinnamon
1 tablespoon ground nutmeg
5 pounds sugar

Peel, core and quarter apples; place in a large kettle. Add enough water to cover apples. Simmer until soft. Stir in the cider, cloves, cinnamon, nutmeg, and sugar. Pour the mixture into a roasting pan; cover. Bake at 350° until the mixture boils; stir occasionally. Lower heat to 250° and bake 5 hours, or overnight. Ladle the apple butter into sterilized jars and seal.

Crispy Corn Sticks

Makes 8 corn sticks.

1 cup cornmeal
¼ teaspoon salt
¼ teaspoon baking soda
3 tablespoons vegetable oil
1 cup buttermilk
1 or 2 tablespoons light corn syrup

Sift cornmeal, salt, and soda. Add oil; stir. Add buttermilk and syrup; mix well. Fill well-greased corn stick pans. Bake at 400° for 30 minutes.

Vermont Maple Custard

3 eggs
½ cup maple syrup
Dash salt
2 cups milk

Beat eggs, syrup, and salt. Blend in milk. Pour into individual cups or molds and place molds in a pan of hot water. Bake at 350° for 40 to 50 minutes or until a knife inserted in center comes out clean.

Celery Supreme

6 cups sliced celery
½ cup water
1 teaspoon salt
1 can sliced water chestnuts, drained
1 2-ounce jar pimiento
½ cup chopped green pepper
1 10¾-ounce can cream of celery or cream of mushroom soup

Combine celery, water, and salt in a large kettle; simmer 10 minutes. Drain. Combine celery mixture, water chestnuts, pimiento, green pepper, and soup in a casserole, stirring gently. Spoon Topping over casserole. Bake at 350° for 20 minutes.

Topping

¼ cup butter, melted
1 cup coarse bread crumbs
½ cup sliced almonds

Combine all ingredients.

Red Cabbage with Raisins

Makes 6 servings.

1 head red cabbage, shredded
¼ cup raisins
½ cup water
½ cup apple juice
2 tablespoons light brown sugar
1½ teaspoons salt
Juice of 1 lemon

Combine all ingredients in a large skillet; cover. Simmer until cabbage is tender and most of the liquid has evaporated.

Hot Percolator Punch

9 cups unsweetened pineapple juice
9 cups cranberry juice
4½ cups water
1 cup brown sugar
4½ teaspoons whole cloves
4 sticks cinnamon, broken
¼ teaspoon salt

Pour first 4 ingredients into a 25-cup coffee pot. In the percolator basket, place spices and salt; perk.

Turkey Casserole

5 or 6 cups diced cooked turkey
½ cup margarine
¾ cup chopped celery
1 onion, chopped
3 cups bread crumbs
1 teaspoon salt
¼ teaspoon baking powder
¼ teaspoon black pepper
¼ teaspoon poultry seasoning
1 egg
1 10¾-ounce can cream of mushroom soup
¾ cup broth or milk

Place turkey in a large casserole. Melt the margarine in a large skillet and sauté the celery, onion, and bread crumbs. Add salt, baking powder, pepper, and poultry seasoning. Beat the egg; combine egg, soup, broth or milk, and crumb mixture. Pour over turkey. Bake, uncovered, at 350° for 45 to 60 minutes.

Christmas Treats

Two-Tone Cookie Slices

Makes 7 dozen.

Dark Mixture

      3 cups sifted flour
      1 teaspoon baking soda
      ¼ teaspoon salt
      ½ teaspoon ground cinnamon
      ½ teaspoon ground cloves
      1 cup shortening, softened
    1½ cups dark brown sugar
      2 eggs
      1 cup finely chopped nuts
      1 cup raisins

Sift together flour, soda, salt, and spices; set aside. Cream shortening with brown sugar; add eggs. Beat well. Stir in dry ingredients, nuts and raisins.

Light Mixture

      2 cups sifted flour
      ½ teaspoon salt
      ¼ teaspoon baking soda
      ½ cup shortening, softened
      ¾ cup sugar
      1 egg
      1 teaspoon vanilla extract
      2 tablespoons water
      ¼ cup chopped candied cherries

Sift together flour, salt, and soda; set aside. Cream shortening and sugar. Add egg, vanilla, and water; mix well. Blend in dry ingredients. Stir in cherries.

Pack half of dark mixture into a waxed paper-lined, straight-sided 10½ x 3½-inch pan or loaf pan. Add all light dough to make a second layer; top with remaining dark dough. Pack firmly. Refrigerate 24 hours. Cut dough in half lengthwise; cut into ¼-inch slices. Bake on ungreased baking sheets at 400° for 8 to 10 minutes. Remove immediately.

Holly Cookies

      6 tablespoons margarine
     24 large marshmallows
      ½ teaspoon vanilla extract
        Green food coloring
    2½ cups cornflakes

Melt all ingredients except cornflakes in the top of a double boiler or over low heat. Pour mixture over cornflakes; fold until entire mixture is colored green. Drop by teaspoonfuls onto waxed paper. Decorate with small cinnamon candies, if desired.

Christmas Trees

      2 9½-ounce packages refrigerated cinnamon rolls
        with icing, prepared according to
        package directions
      6 tablespoons chopped candied mixed fruit

Arrange rolls on a greased baking sheet in rows to simulate a Christmas tree. Bake in a preheated 375° oven for 18 to 20 minutes. Remove from baking sheet onto a large platter or breadboard or cut cardboard which has been covered with foil. While rolls are hot, spread with icing and sprinkle with fruit to decorate.

Poinsettia Cookies

Makes about 5 dozen.

      2 cups confectioners' sugar
      1 cup butter or margarine, softened
      2 eggs
      1 teaspoon vanilla extract
      ½ teaspoon rum extract
      3 cups flour
      1 teaspoon salt
      1 cup shredded coconut
      1 cup butterscotch chips
        Granulated sugar
      ½ cup candied red cherries, cut in wedges

Cream confectioners' sugar and butter; add eggs and extracts. Sift together flour and salt; stir into butter mixture. Stir in coconut and ¾ cup of the butterscotch chips. Chill dough until firm. Roll into 1-inch balls. Place on ungreased baking sheets. Flatten cookie with the bottom of a glass dipped in granulated sugar. Place a butterscotch chip in the center of each cookie. Place cherry wedges in a circle to resemble a poinsettia. Bake at 375° for about 12 minutes.

Kris Kringles

Makes 40 slices.

- 1 6-ounce package semisweet chocolate chips
- 2 tablespoons butter or margarine
- 1 egg
- 1 cup sifted confectioners' sugar
  Dash salt
- ½ teaspoon vanilla extract
- ½ cup flaked coconut
- ½ cup chopped dry roasted peanuts

In a medium saucepan, melt chocolate and butter over low heat, stirring constantly. Remove from heat; cool to lukewarm. Beat in egg until smooth and glossy. Add confectioners' sugar, salt, and vanilla; mix well. Stir in coconut and nuts. Chill. Form into a 10-inch-long roll. Wrap and chill until firm, several hours or overnight. Slice ¼ inch thick.

Holiday Divinity

- 2 egg whites
- 1 3-ounce package fruit-flavored gelatin
- 3 cups sugar
- ¾ cup light corn syrup
- ¾ cup water

Beat egg whites until light. Add gelatin and beat until stiff. Cook remaining ingredients. Stir until mixture reaches hard ball stage (250° on a candy thermometer). Beat in the egg whites and pour into a buttered 8-inch square pan. Cool. Cut into squares.

Pecan Pralines

- 2 cups white sugar
- 1 cup brown sugar
- 1 tablespoon butter
- ½ cup milk
- 3 cups pecans

Combine first 4 ingredients and bring to a boil. Add pecans and cook 4 minutes. Remove from heat and drop by spoonfuls onto waxed paper.

Date-Walnut Pinwheel Cookies

Makes 4 dozen.

- 1 cup chopped dates
- ½ teaspoon grated lemon rind
- ½ teaspoon lemon juice
- ½ cup water
- ½ cup sugar
- 1 cup chopped walnuts
- 1 13-ounce package plain cookie mix
- 1 egg, beaten
- 1 tablespoon water

Combine dates, lemon rind, lemon juice, ½ cup water, and sugar in a saucepan. Cook about 10 minutes, stirring until thick. Add walnuts. Cool. Blend cookie mix with egg and the 1 tablespoon water. Roll in 2 10 x 7-inch rectangles. Spread with walnut and date mixture. Roll up jelly-roll fashion. Wrap in waxed paper; chill until firm. Slice ¼-inch thick. Bake on a greased baking sheet at 375° for 8 to 9 minutes.

Note: These rolls can be frozen. Slice frozen and bake.

Two-Flavored Fudge

Makes about 2½ pounds.

- 2 cups firmly packed brown sugar
- 1 cup sugar
- 1 cup evaporated milk
- ½ cup butter
- 1 7-ounce jar marshmallow creme
- 1 6-ounce package butterscotch chips
- 1 6-ounce package semisweet chocolate chips
- 1 cup chopped walnuts
- 1 teaspoon vanilla extract

In a saucepan combine first 4 ingredients. Bring to a full boil over moderate heat, stirring frequently. Boil 15 minutes over moderate heat, stirring occasionally. Remove from heat. Add marshmallow creme, butterscotch chips, and chocolate chips. Stir until chips are melted and mixture is smooth. Blend in walnuts and vanilla. Pour into a greased 9-inch square pan. Chill until firm.

Peanut Butter Candy

    3 cups sugar
    ⅛ teaspoon salt
    1 cup milk
    2 tablespoons butter
    1 cup peanut butter
    1 teaspoon vanilla extract

Combine sugar, salt, and milk in a 2-quart sauce-pan. Quickly bring to a boil, stirring only until sugar is dissolved. Boil, without stirring, until mixture reaches soft ball stage (234° on a candy thermometer). Remove from heat and add butter, peanut butter, and vanilla. Mix thoroughly. Pour into buttered 8-inch square pan. When cool, cut into pieces.

Oatmeal Fruit Cookies

    ¾ cup butter or margarine, softened
    1 cup packed brown sugar
    2 eggs
    2 cups whole wheat flour
    1 cup rolled oats
    ½ teaspoon baking soda
    1 teaspoon baking powder
    1 teaspoon ground cinnamon
    ¼ cup milk
    1 cup chopped candied cherries or mixed fruit
    1 cup chopped pecans or walnuts

Cream butter, sugar, and eggs until well blended. Combine dry ingredients; add to butter and egg mixture. Mix well. Add enough milk to make the dough easy to handle. Mix in fruits and nuts. Drop by teaspoonfuls onto a greased baking sheet. Bake at 350° for 8 to 12 minutes or until browned.

Cinnamon Crisps

    ½ pound butter, softened
    1 cup sugar
    1 egg
    3 cups flour
    ½ teaspoon salt
    1½ teaspoons ground cinnamon
    1 teaspoon baking powder

Cream butter and sugar until light and fluffy. Add egg; beat well. Sift together flour, salt, cinnamon, and baking powder. Add to creamed mixture. Chill about 1 hour for easy handling. Roll out on a floured board to ⅛-inch thickness; cut into desired shapes. Place on ungreased baking sheets. Bake at 350° for 11 to 12 minutes or until light brown. Remove cookies from baking sheet immediately. Cool on wire racks. Store in an airtight container.

Mock Fondant Balls

    ½ cup butter, softened
    1 pound confectioners' sugar
    ¼ cup heavy cream
    1 teaspoon vanilla extract
       Hazelnuts, pecans or walnuts
       Candied fruit, chopped

Cream butter until light; gradually add sugar. When very thick add cream and vanilla a little at a time. Turn out on a board sprinkled with confectioners' sugar; knead. Break off about 2 teaspoons of the mixture and place around a nutmeat or piece of candied fruit to form a ball. Roll in confectioners' sugar. Repeat with remaining dough. Store in an airtight container in refrigerator.

Melt-in-the-Mouth Caramels

Makes about 2½ pounds.

    1 cup butter or margarine
    1 pound brown sugar
       Dash salt
    1 cup light corn syrup
    1 15-ounce can sweetened condensed milk
    1 teaspoon vanilla extract

Melt butter in a heavy 3-quart saucepan. Add brown sugar and salt. Stir until thoroughly combined. Stir in corn syrup; mix well. Gradually add milk, stirring constantly. Cook and stir over medium heat until candy reaches firm ball stage (245° on candy thermometer), about 12 to 15 minutes. Remove from heat. Stir in vanilla. Pour into buttered 9-inch square pan. Cool and cut into squares.

Yuletide Casserole

    2 3-ounce cans whole mushrooms, drained,
       reserve liquid
    2 tablespoons butter
    ½ teaspoon paprika
    2½ cups diced cooked ham
       Chicken broth
    2 10¾-ounce cans cream of chicken soup, undiluted
    6 hard-cooked eggs
       Pimiento
       Parsley

Sauté mushrooms in butter and paprika a few minutes. Add ham and sauté 2 minutes. Add enough chicken broth to mushroom liquid to make ¾ cup. Stir in mushroom liquid and soup; simmer over low heat, stirring, until smooth and hot. Separate 1 hard-cooked egg yolk from the white; set aside. Quarter egg white and remaining eggs and fold into ham mixture. Garnish with crumbled reserved egg yolk, pimiento, and parsley. Serve immediately with Saffron Rice with Peas.

Note: Casserole may be cooled, covered and refrigerated overnight if desired. Reheat at low temperature before serving.

Saffron Rice with Peas

Cook 6 servings of rice in water seasoned with powdered saffron to taste. Cook 1 10-ounce package frozen peas; drain. Fold into rice.

Dinner Rolls

    1 package dry yeast
    ½ cup warm water (110 to 115°)
    ½ cup scalded milk
    ¼ cup butter
    2 tablespoons sugar
    1½ teaspoons salt
    1 egg
    3 cups sifted flour

Dissolve yeast in water; set aside. Combine milk, butter, sugar, and salt. Add yeast mixture; mix well. Blend in the egg. Gradually add flour. Mix until dough is well blended and soft. Shape dough into rolls on a well-floured board. Let rise in a warm place until double in bulk. Bake at 350° for 15 to 20 minutes or until done.

Note: If dough is to be chilled, place in a greased bowl, cover, and refrigerate at least 2 hours. Remove and let rise in a warm place until double in bulk, about 1½ to 2 hours. Bake as above.

German Christmas Stollen

Makes 1 stollen.

    ¾ cup milk, scalded
    ¼ cup sugar
    ½ teaspoon salt
    ¼ cup butter or margarine
    ¼ cup warm water (110 to 115°)
    1 package dry yeast
    2¾ cups unsifted flour
    ⅛ teaspoon ground cardamom
    ½ cup seedless raisins
    ¼ cup chopped citron
    ½ cup chopped pecans
    1 tablespoon butter or margarine, melted

To the scalded milk, add sugar, salt, and butter. Cool to lukewarm. Measure warm water into a large, warm bowl. Add yeast; stir until dissolved. Add lukewarm milk mixture, 2 cups of the flour and cardamom. Beat until smooth. Stir in remaining flour, raisins, citron, and pecans. Turn out on a lightly floured board and knead until smooth and elastic, about 5 minutes. Place in a greased bowl, turning to grease top. Cover. Let rise in a warm place until double in bulk, about 1 hour. Roll dough into an oblong shape about ½ inch thick. Brush with melted butter. Fold in half lengthwise. Place on a greased baking sheet; cover. Let rise in a warm place until double in bulk, about 45 minutes. Bake at 350° about 40 minutes. Ice with Confectioners' Sugar Frosting.

Confectioners' Sugar Frosting

    1 cup confectioners' sugar
    1 to 2 tablespoons hot milk or water

In a small bowl, add milk or water gradually to sugar. Blend until mixture is smooth; spread over stollen. Decorate stollen with candied cherries and nuts if desired.

Fruitcake

- 1 pound candied citron
- 8 ounces raisins
- 12 ounces green and red candied cherries, chopped
- 1 pound pecans, chopped
- 1 pound dates, chopped
- 4 ounces almond halves
- ¼ cup flour

Toss all ingredients together until well blended. Set aside and mix Batter.

Batter

- 1 cup shortening, softened
- ½ cup sugar
- ½ cup brown sugar
- ½ cup honey
- 5 eggs, beaten
- 1½ cups flour
- 1 teaspoon salt
- 3 teaspoons baking powder
- 1 teaspoon ground cinnamon
- ½ teaspoon ground allspice
- ½ teaspoon ground cloves
- ½ teaspoon ground nutmeg

Cream shortening and sugars well. Add honey and eggs, mixing after each addition. Sift dry ingredients together; add to creamed mixture. Pour Batter over fruit mixture and mix thoroughly. Line greased tube pan with brown paper; grease paper. Bake at 250° over a pan of water for 4 hours. Cool in pan; remove. Pour about 1 cup fruit juice or brandy over top as desired. Wrap in foil and store in the refrigerator.

Note: If desired, decorate with cherries and almonds, using almonds for flower petals and cherries for centers.

Holly Wreath Pie

- 2 envelopes unflavored gelatin
- ¼ cup sugar
- 4 cups eggnog
- 1 cup whipping cream, whipped
- ½ cup chopped maraschino cherries
- ½ cup chopped nuts
- 1 baked pastry shell
  Green citron
  Red maraschino cherries

Combine gelatin and sugar in the top of a double boiler. Stir in 1 cup of the eggnog. Place over boiling water; stir until gelatin and sugar are dissolved. Remove from heat. Add remaining eggnog. Chill to consistency of unbeaten egg white. Whip until light and fluffy. Fold in the whipped cream, chopped cherries, and nuts. Turn into baked pie shell. Chill until firm. To decorate, make small holly wreaths of citron, cut into quarter-moon shapes and placed on top of filling to form rings. Place a tiny piece of red maraschino cherry in the centers.

English Mincemeat

- 1 pound dried currants, rinsed
- 1 pound seedless raisins, rinsed
- 3 large apples, chopped with skins
- 1 pound mixed fruit peel
- 2 teaspoons salt
- 1 pound suet, chopped
  Juice and grated peel of 1 lemon
- 1 pound brown sugar
  Ground nutmeg, allspice and cinnamon to taste

Combine all ingredients; mix thoroughly. Pour into a large covered jar. Store in refrigerator.

Mincemeat Cookies

Makes 5½ dozen.

- 3¼ cups flour
- ½ teaspoon salt
- 1 teaspoon baking soda
- 1 cup shortening, softened
- 1½ cups sugar
- 3 eggs, well beaten
- 1⅓ cups prepared mincemeat

Sift flour, salt, and baking soda; set aside. Cream shortening and sugar until smooth. Beat in the eggs. Stir in mincemeat. Add flour mixture, mixing well. Drop by teaspoonfuls, 2 inches apart, onto a greased baking sheet. Bake at 400° for 12 minutes.

Festive Eggnog Cake

Makes 1 9-inch layer cake.

    2 cups flour
    1½ cups sugar
    1 tablespoon baking powder
    1 teaspoon salt
    ¼ teaspoon ground nutmeg
    3 eggs
    1 teaspoon vanilla extract
    1 cup eggnog
    ½ cup butter, softened

Combine all ingredients in a large mixing bowl. Blend well at low speed of electric mixer. Grease and flour the bottoms of 2 9-inch pans; pour batter into pans. Bake at 350° for 25 to 30 minutes or until cake springs back when lightly touched in center. Cool. Fill and frost with Eggnog Frosting.

Eggnog Frosting

    ¼ cup flour
    ¼ teaspoon salt
    1 cup eggnog
    ⅔ cup butter, softened
    1 cup sugar
    1 teaspoon vanilla extract

Combine flour, salt, and eggnog in a small saucepan. Cook over low heat, stirring constantly, until very thick. Cool. Gradually cream butter and sugar. Add flour mixture; beat until light and fluffy. Blend in vanilla.

Marmalade Noel

Makes 7 to 8 jars.

    3 oranges
    1 lemon
    2 cups crushed pineapple, drained
    3 pounds sugar
    ½ cup hot water
    1 bottle maraschino cherries, drained

Wash oranges and lemon; peel very thin. Scrape white from peel and remove all membrane. Chop fruit and peels or grind in food chopper. Add pineapple, sugar, and water. Boil slowly for ½ hour. Add cherries. Pour into jars and seal with paraffin.

Traditional Suet Cake

    2 teaspoons baking soda
    1⅓ cups sour milk or buttermilk
    1 cup molasses
    ⅔ cup sugar
    2 eggs, lightly beaten
    3 cups flour
    1 teaspoon baking powder
    2 teaspoons ground cinnamon
    2 teaspoons ground ginger
    2 cups chopped suet
    2 cups chopped nuts
    2 cups chopped dates or raisins, dusted with flour

Dissolve soda in sour milk; set aside. Mix molasses, sugar, and eggs in a large mixing bowl. In a separate bowl sift together dry ingredients. Alternately add with sour milk and soda mixture. Add suet, nuts, and floured dates or raisins. Pour into a 9 x 13-inch greased and floured pan. Bake at 275° for 30 to 40 minutes. Serve warm with whipped cream or a lemon sauce.

Charlotte Russe

Makes 10 to 12 servings.

    2 envelopes unflavored gelatin
    ¼ cup water
    4 eggs, separated
    1 cup sugar
    1 pint milk
    ½ teaspoon cream of tartar
    1 pint whipping cream
    1 teaspoon vanilla extract
       Confectioners' sugar to taste
    1 sponge cake

Dissolve gelatin in the water over low heat. Cool. Beat egg yolks. Gradually beat in ¾ cup of the sugar. Add milk. Cook in the top of a double boiler over low heat until mixture thickens slightly. Stir in gelatin. Cool. Stir until smooth. Beat egg whites and cream of tartar until mixture forms soft peaks. Gradually add the remaining ¼ cup sugar, beating until stiff. Fold into custard. Whip cream with vanilla; add confectioners' sugar. Fold into custard. Break cake into pieces in dessert dishes. Pour custard over. Refrigerate overnight.

Black Forest Cherry Cake

Makes 8 servings.

- 4 eggs
- ¾ teaspoon vanilla extract
- ⅔ cup sugar
- ⅓ cup cocoa
- ⅓ cup sifted flour
- 6 tablespoons butter, melted
- ½ cup sugar
- ¾ cup water
- ¼ cup kirsch
- ⅓ cup confectioners' sugar
- 2 cups whipping cream, whipped
- 1 cup pitted dark cherries, drained
  Maraschino cherries
- 1 4-ounce bar semisweet chocolate, shaved
  into curls

Combine eggs, vanilla, and the ⅔ cup sugar; beat with electric mixer 10 minutes at high speed. Sift together flour and cocoa; fold into egg mixture. Add melted butter, stirring just until mixed. Do not overmix. Pour into 3 greased and floured 8-inch round pans. Bake at 350° for 10 to 15 minutes. Cool 5 minutes. Remove from pans and cool on racks. In a saucepan, combine the ½ cup sugar and water; boil 5 minutes. Cool to luke-warm and add kirsch. Sprinkle over cake layers. Fold confectioners' sugar into whipped cream. Spread on one cake layer; top with half of the cherries. Repeat with second layer; then add top layer. Frost top and sides of cake with remaining whipped cream and garnish with maraschino cherries and shaved chocolate.

Pretzel Torte

- 2½ cups crushed pretzel sticks with
  some salt removed
- ½ cup butter, melted
- ¾ cup sugar
- 2 3-ounce packages cream cheese, softened
- ½ cup confectioners' sugar
- 2 packages nondairy whipped topping, prepared
- 1 21-ounce can cherry pie filling

Mix 2 cups of the crushed pretzels, butter, and sugar together; press into a 9 x 13-inch pan. Bake at 350° for 5 to 10 minutes. Remove from oven and cool. Mix cream cheese with confec-tioners' sugar. Fold whipped topping into cheese mixture and spread on baked crust. Pour cherry pie filling over mixture. Sprinkle the remaining ½ cup pretzel crumbs on top. Refrigerate overnight.

Cherry Squares

- 1 cup sugar
- 1 cup flour
- 1 teaspoon ground cinnamon
- 1 teaspoon baking soda
- 1 egg
- 1 cup chopped nuts
- 3½ cups canned bing cherries, drained, reserve juice
- 2 tablespoons butter, melted

Mix ingredients in order given. Bake in a 9-inch square pan at 325° for 45 minutes. Serve topped with Sauce and a dollop of whipped cream.

Cherry Sauce

- Cherry juice
- ⅓ cup sugar
- 1 tablespoon cornstarch mixed with cold water
- 1 tablespoon butter

Heat cherry juice in a saucepan. Add sugar and cornstarch mixture. Add butter; stir to blend. Cool until thickened.

Carrot Cake with Pineapple

- 3 eggs, lightly beaten
- 2 cups sugar
- 1⅓ cups vegetable oil
- 3 cups flour
- 1 teaspoon salt
- 2 teaspoons baking soda
- 2 teaspoons ground cinnamon
- 2 cups grated carrots
- 1 cup chopped walnuts or pecans
- 1 cup drained, crushed pineapple
- 2 teaspoons vanilla extract

Blend eggs, sugar, and oil. Sift together flour, salt, soda, and cinnamon. Stir in egg mixture, carrots, nuts, pineapple, and vanilla. Pour batter into an ungreased 10-inch tube pan. Bake at 350° for 1 hour and 15 minutes. Cool cake right-side up for 25 minutes; then loosen around sides. Ice with a lemon glaze.

Index